D1399668

Free Gondola Ride

A summer with the men
behind the mystery

by

Kathleen Ann González

González, Kathleen Ann, 1965-
Free Gondola Ride / by Kathleen Ann González

ISBN:0-615-12391-0

Printed in the United States.

Front cover artwork by Dino DeZorzi.
Cover layout and book formating by RJ Wofford II.

Author's Note
All stories told in this work are based on personal experience and interviews with those portrayed. In some instances the names and identifying details have been changed.

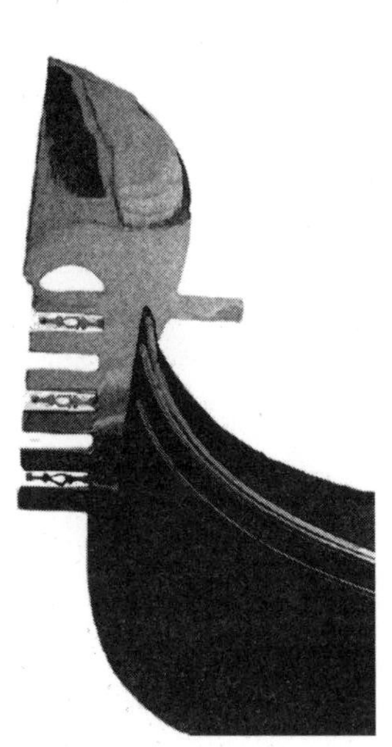

Table of Contents

Acknowledgements 9

Preface 11

1. The Degenerating Interview 15
2. Gramoe 29
3. An Exhibition of Strength and Fearlessness 37
4. The Fraglia 41
5. Rescued by Cappuccino 49
6. Double Happiness 57
7. The Red Cucumber 61
8. Il Casanova Moderno 71
9. A Different Breed 77
10. Il Lovo Uomo 87
11. Cuckold's Horns 92
12. Full Moon Glide 99
13. Dead Dog 113

14. Peste Turistica 118

15. Bella Bella Bella 123

16. Lino's Livingroom 129

17. Italian Lessons 137

18. I Tre Amici 145

19. Don't Tell My Brother 151

20. The Remer 159

21. No More Prosecco, Pastries, or Panini 163

22. Invitations and Scoldings 169

23. Chicken Innards 181

24. Fandango 193

25. Saying Goodbye 204

A Short History of the Gondola 215

Glossary 231

Bibliography 236

Acknowledgements

A friend once said to me, "All we have are our dreams. We have to help each other make them come true." I'm so fortunate and honored to have people to thank for their contributions to my dream.

First and foremost, I must thank the gondoliers of Venice: Max and Rico, whose conversations inspired the idea, Stefano whose continued friendship has kept Venice alive for me, and the many men within these pages and many who aren't, whose lives and work color this volume. They probably don't know how their "Ciao, bellas!" and kisses brought me back to myself. I hope I have done them justice and that they find joy in these pages.

If it takes a village to raise a child, it takes a tribe to revise a book. I owe a debt to my writing group—the Scribe Tribe—for their invaluable advice, guidance, and readings. Usha Alexander, Jason Cabassi, John Cavanaugh, Susanna Dyer, and Chad McDonald: fondue for you!

Numerous other friends have given generously of

their time and opinions to help bring this project to fruition and buoy my spirits during the long process. A round of fragolino to Karen Morvay, Heather Jones, Michael McCarthy, Brian Lew, Gil and Rita González, Gary and Taffy González, Eric Lambart, Norma Howe, Clarence Robert Tower, and others who read early drafts. Also a special thanks to Dino DeZorzi and his wonderful wife Angela for their fast and fancy footwork while designing the cover.

Finally, a gondola-load of gratitude goes to RJ Wofford, without whom this book could not have been created. His countless hours designing the cover art, formatting the book, tracking down answers and details, encouraging me when I'd be down, and keeping my dream alive cannot be repaid. I needed someone to stand beside me for this book to be made, and there he was, helping my dream come true.

Preface

In this book, I set out to discover what life is like for the gondoliers of Venice: the best days and the worst, the good customers and the bad, and the day-to-day adventures. Haven't people romanticized these men beyond reason? Turned them into cliches? Or ignored them like a taxi driver? Besides the guidebook description or brief article, I found that no one had examined the gondolier and his craft. I had intended to interview them as a proper journalist would, notepad and tape recorder by my side, but I found that interviewing a group of casanovas was easier said than done. In typical Italian fashion, things were rarely straight to the point; conversations were as circuitous as Venetian canals, and details were haggled over like a crate of tomatoes. Generally, what I intended to be an interview with a single gondolier degenerated into a collection of comments from all present, flying from English to Italian to Venetian dialect to Spanish. Jokes flowed freely, sometimes at my expense.

The resulting chapters are not always separate

interviews with individual gondoliers but instead may be my days spent in the company of their groups or my being propositioned by a lone wolf. Sometimes I gleaned specific facts from the whole, while other encounters showed more about a gondolier's character than about his profession.

Paul Theroux once wrote, "...travel was flight and pursuit in equal parts." While trying to interview these men, I pursued a goal, yet to my surprise found that I was engaged in a personal dance of flight and pursuit. This colored my encounters with the gondoliers more than I would have imagined.

If you wish to start with the facts, read the chapter "A Short History of the Gondola" at the back of this book. Or simply dive into the canal headfirst and fill in those blanks later.

Legend, mystery, and intrigue have encircled the gondoliers and their vessels for ages. This book aims to uncover the men behind the mystique: their personalities and peculiarities, their virtues and vices, their features and foibles. I invite you to get to know the gondoliers of Venice, and as the old barcarolle goes, "Come with me, we shall get into the gondola and go forth on the sea."

Giannino, Stefano, Diego, and Max while away the afternoon at the Santa Sofia traghetto.

The Degenerating Interview

"Gondola! Gondola!" rolled off Max's tongue like a jackpot from a slot machine. The bewildered tourist couple, who had wandered over to look at the Grand Canal, quickly shook their heads and scurried off, the woman clutching her purse to her side. Max had interrupted our conversation with his hawker's cry, and now he turned back to me, though not for long.

Giannino strode over and grabbed my hand, turning my palm upwards and foretelling that I would fall in love with him. Max swatted at Giannino's leg like he was shooing a fly, and Venetian words flew between them, jokingly berating each other, I guessed by their facial expressions. An older gondolier hindered the conversation further by sweeping under Max's chair. The guys commenced yelling at each other in dialect. Gondolier number four arrived with a bag of melons, while number five grabbed a knife, and they all stood to eat their slices, ignoring me completely until someone handed me some cantaloupe.

How was I to conduct an interview amidst this melee?

When I first conceived the idea of writing a book about Venice's gondoliers, I pictured myself as the studious journalist, sitting before a focused gondolier, writing a serious book about their lives. After doing some research, I found that very little had been written about these men, so I pledged to take it on. The previous summer, on my second trip to Venice, I had been befriended (well, hit on is closer to the truth) by Max, a gondolier at the Santa Sofia gondolier station, or traghetto. After a few conversations with him and another gondolier named Rico, I became more intrigued by their job and lifestyle, not to mention the gondola's lengthy history. Little did I know how my plans would be so shaped by that very job and lifestyle and the men who manned the traghetto.

"I start work at eight o'clock tomorrow," Max told me when I saw him on my first day back in Venice. "What time do you come?"

"Nine?" I ventured, not wanting to appear overeager.

"But I start at eight," he repeated, then with a shrug added, "but I will be there all day."

I felt like we had made some sort of appointment. Max had agreed to help me interview some of the gondoliers as they worked at the Santa Sofia traghetto stop, where they ferried people across the Grand Canal or took tourists on private rides. Max had charmed me with his good looks and carefree manner. He still had the dark tan and ubiquitous sunglasses that I remembered from the previous year, which hid his startling green eyes. But this year he had begun wearing his black sideburns to a sharp point halfway across his cheek, apparently a newly popular style. He went by Max or Massimo or Campagna, a gondolier nickname that meant "Country," signifying that he lived on the mainland. Luckily for me, Max was well known and well liked by fellow gondoliers, so he offered me a foot in the door to meet more subjects to interview.

However, when I crept tentatively towards the traghetto just after nine that morning, armed with two cameras, a tape recorder, and pads of paper, Max was not to be found. Walking down the wide, empty campo towards the canal and dock, I felt overexposed, too obviously a woman tourist, not enough the studious journalist. I stood indecisively under the wooden trellis, sheltered from the sun by the trees and vines entwined above me. "Maybe he is at breakfast," offered one man from his boat. I ventured off in search of cappuccino at Bar Lucciola, my neighborhood haunt, before returning to find that Max would not appear until one o'clock.

But Max wasn't really starting work even then. Instead he treated me to lunch at Trattoria alla Madonna, and wine, and small talk until I wondered if this would be a wasted day. I was anxious to start my project. But here in the restaurant with simple wooden tables and white-aproned waiters, Max was more interested in making sure that I had plenty to eat, ordering for me an insalata mista, shrimp, pasta, and soave, a light local white wine, and then still plying me with forkfuls from his own plate. "Here," he'd say with his fork dangling pasta, "you try mine. It's very good." He was using this maneuver as a flirtation, but it was one which I didn't mind. Some foods always taste better off a handsome man's plate, and my boyfriend back home hadn't been feeding me from his plate in a while.

Finally, over coffee, I thought I'd change the conversation's direction and make the mood more professional by showing Max the magazine story I had written the previous year, which featured him, his partner Giannino, and other gondoliers I had met then. He flipped through it too quickly to read anything, pausing longer at the photos of himself and Giannino, (though later he betrayed a greater interest when we returned to the traghetto and he immediately showed the photos to the nearest gondolier). While Max's spoken English was generally sufficient, he was self-taught, and it dawned on me that his ability to read English might be lacking. I remembered one time I had been applying lipstick and he had lifted his chin, saying, "Oh, the lapstick." It took me a moment to realize that he wasn't making a lewd suggestion. Who knew what his reading skills were like?

Then he set me straight on some of the details in the magazine article. "This Giannino," he said, jabbing a finger at the name on the page. "It is spelled with two 'n's' here." Great, I thought, I've already disrespected his partner. "Opulent gondola?" he questioned next, regarding the caption below a photograph I had taken. "Nooo, this is not a gondola."

It certainly wasn't a ship or a kayak; this black, narrow boat replete with cushions and lace appeared to be the real article. "Is a sandolo fixed to look like the gondola, but is not the real thing," he said as he pointed to the picture. "Some people try to say this is the gondola so they get the money from the tourists." He went on to explain that for the real gondola, a boatman had to pass a test and get a license to drive it. It was all very regulated.

As Max turned to the last page of my story, he saw a photo of the ferro, the curved silver ornament on the front of a gondola. "This is not really the ferro," he commented, leaning back and turning down the corners of his mouth. Now, that had been something that all my sources had agreed on, so I was quite stunned. "For Venetians and for gondoliers, it is the fero, but only with one 'r'," he explained. "For the outsiders, it is called the rostro." At this point I realized that casual conversation wouldn't do after all, and I had better grab my paper and pen to record my facts correctly. I also realized that while I was feeling increasingly stupid, Max was probably feeling increasingly smart, making him more willing to share his world with me.

While Max talked about the fero, he also provided many more details that I had never seen in any book. He leaned towards me as he pointed to my photo and explained the symbolism. Besides the six forward-facing prongs that represented the sestieri (Venice's districts) and Giudecca island, the backward "S" shape of the fero followed the curves of the Grand Canal. The wide arc of silver at the top mimicked the shape of the doge's, or governor's, hat, and finally, the three more-intricately carved prongs between those of the sestieri stood for the larger of the outlying islands: Murano, Burano, and Torcello. The arch beneath the doge's hat represented the Rialto Bridge. That one hunk of iron symbolized many major events and places within the Venetian lagoon.

After that, I started plying Max with direct questions—factual details that my printed sources had left out or that were contradictory. "How many gondoliers work in Venice? How many gondolas still exist? What does it take to become a gondolier?" Here I had hit pay dirt with Max because he enjoyed talking about a subject on which he was an expert. He suddenly became quite business-like, his charm scurrying underground. Being a third-generation gondolier, Max had much to say on the subject. He had practically grown up on a gondola, his father teaching him the craft as a boy and using him as an assistant. Max seemed to embrace the entire gondolier mystique: a womanizer, a macho man, handsome, generous, hardworking while supremely fun-loving. He enjoyed dressing the part and always donned his straw hat while others often ditched theirs.

Answering my first question was easy. "There are exactly 403 gondoliers in Venice," recited Max. He went on to explain that each year, some gondoliers left the profession, and only that number of openings were available. Newcomers faced stiff competition. For example, when Max started eleven years before at age eighteen, there were eight openings and 895 applicants. I congratulated him on having made it into the ranks, though I wondered if the fact that his father was a gondolier played a part in his success.

"The test is two parts," he explained. "First, you have to row the gondola while judges look at you to see your form, see how strong you are and so on. You earn points for this."

"And is there a written test also?" I inquired.

"Yes, they want to see how well you know the history of the gondola, the parts of Venice, see if you can speak English," he offered, adding hand gestures like ticking off a list. "You earn the points for this, too." Max explained that each gondolier had a license to operate his boat, but if he wanted to go on vacation, someone else with a permit could operate it temporarily. Some men were licensed only as traghetto workers or substitutes, of which there were no limit. Max proudly owned his boat, which cost him about the price of a Mercedes. I later learned that new gondolas ranged between twenty and sixty thousand dollars, depending on their level of opulence.

Once we returned to the shaded patio of the Santa Sofia traghetto stop, my story and photos were passed around and simultaneously a deck of cards came out. The Santa Sofia traghetto, across from the Pescheria or fish market, is one of eight small boat docks on the Grand Canal where people can take a traghetto boat—a sort of large, plain gondola—across the Grand Canal. The traghetto refers to both the larger gondola-shaped boat and the station, and it provides a necessary canal-crossing service since there are only three bridges spanning the Grand Canal. Locals are the most avid users of this ancient convenience. Gondoliers man these stations all day, with apparently plenty of free time in between shifts. Besides the pier for the traghetto boat, another two piers allowed for private gondola access. A boathouse, known as a casotto in dialect, some tables, and chairs provided the gondoliers with their home for the day.

The seven gondoliers not rowing the traghetto boat at the moment chattered on, joking in dialect, playing cards, gesticulating. Some sat in the plastic chairs arranged at a table while others stood in the wooden house where their belongings were stored. They looked like club members in their matching black slacks and requisite shirts: white, red and white striped, or blue and white striped. I felt like a tolerated outsider, a tourist who had stayed longer than her 50-minute gondola ride, and wondered how I would find a way into their world.

As I checked out the gondoliers sprawled around the place, I noticed that today only Stefano wore his straw hat but with the ribbons tucked inside, "Because they itch," he explained, scratching his arm in demonstration. Max had introduced me to Stefano right away, thinking Stefano could help me with research because his English was quite good. Along with Max and Giannino, Stefano was one of the senior gondoliers on this shift. Stefano was in his late twenties, younger than his brother Giannino, yet he seemed more mature and stable. I immediately felt like I could trust him, maybe because a pick-up line wasn't the first thing out of his mouth. Yet Stefano also harbored a playful side with his jokes and his blond-tipped hair betraying its darker roots. This day (as on many, I was to find), he had chosen to let his scraggly beard grow. He had a quick and infectious smile. As I got to know him, his smile warmed me with its sincerity and friendliness. "Later," he said, "my wife, she comes by with our baby. Maybe you get to see them."

When I joined the group at the white plastic table, Paolo turned to me. He was a stocky man, suntanned like the rest of them, and with a scar on his upper lip. Paolo worked the traghetto only and was not a full-time gondolier; he held this job for its good money while he finished his education to become a radiology technician. "Ask me the questions because I speak better English than him," he insisted, hooking his thumb towards Max. I was grateful because the torrent of Venetian the men poured out sounded like water over rocks to my unaccustomed ears. Though I had generally understood Max, I was to discover that Paolo could speak at a more complex level of understanding, helping me to fill in gaps or decipher misunderstandings.

I took out my list while Paolo cocked his head and read bits of it upside down across the table. "How many gondolas still exist?" he read, and thus ensued between the men a lot of conjecture in Venetian dialect, a rapid-fire speech from "O" shaped mouths. None of the men could agree on the number of gondolas still around except that it was more than 403.

The question of how many years a gondola lasts triggered more dialect. Max and Stefano started to tell me that the first gondola was made in the 12th century, but Paolo stretched out his hand to stop them. "No," he said, looking at me, "I know what you are asking," and he translated it for the others.

"Fifty years," calculated Paolo, "if it has a good owner. But if not, then maybe fifteen years." They explained that the waves of the motorboats, not pollution, were responsible for most of the damage to the hulls. A good owner will keep his boat clean and covered at night and will repaint it on a regular basis. Gondolas need to be scraped free of moss; only a couple boatyards remain to perform this service. Max's father's boat, at his recent retirement, was almost 40 years old.

"What is your next question?" inquired Paolo, one of the few present who was still paying attention to me. He stretched out his arm to snatch the paper from me. Another guy was slouched down in his chair with his head thrown back and his eyes closed. One young gondolier, known as Condom for reasons I didn't want to know, sat silently throughout the entire conversation. Later, the men told me an elaborate tale about this guy being nicknamed for the Venetian playwright Goldoni, which sounded like condom, they averred. With a twinkle in his eye, Max said, "You know, Goldon, condom. . . ." I wasn't buying that piece of rotten prosciutto. Nearby, an older man with gray hair and bushy eyebrows used his straw broom to sweep the wooden walkway to the traghetto. I fell in love at once with the Venetian straw brooms that looked like they had been stolen out from under flying witches. Max and Giannino were absorbed in their card game.

To anyone who was listening, I asked, "How much money does a gondolier earn each year?"

The men suddenly focused more on the card game than on my questions. It was like a scene in an old spaghetti western where the man in black walks out from the shadows of the saloon. "It's private," was all Max would say, while the others tossed cards to the center of the table. I backed off for a bit and let them play, admiring the novel faces of kings and queens on their cards, the primary colors and thick black lines vibrant and striking.

After an interlude of their joking and playing and my silent discomfort, I dove back in with another question. I wasn't one to be easily daunted by silence or discomfort. Trying to sound casual, I asked, "So who was your worst customer?"

No one could think of a single person or group who evoked bad memories. Instead, they all agreed that the French, as a people, were usually the worst. "They say in Venice it is too expensive," offered Stefano. "But one time I made a vacation in Paris, and a bottle of water was, like, 5,000 lire. Here, you go to the market and water costs 600 lire," he concluded, throwing up his hands.

The others spoke all at once, telling of French tourists who didn't want to pay the full price for the gondola ride and yet also wanted it to last longer. Many didn't even want to pay the 700 lire (about 47 cents) for the traghetto crossing. "Some of these people dress nice—nice pants, nice shoes—but complain about the cost," Paolo added.

As I prompted them again about good or bad customers, Paolo offered to name the worst gondolier he had heard of—Virgilio—who was now retired.

Max, who had known Virgilio, said that in the past, the older gondoliers were more close-minded, while the younger men now were more open, which he illustrated with hands held away from his head. "If a gondolier was late one minute to the job, Virgilio would send him home for the day," Max explained. "And in the morning he would not even say 'buon giorno.'" Here, Max made a sour face to illustrate Virgilio's black moods. Max was friends with everyone, and contemplating someone so stern set him on edge.

At this point, the gondoliers began interviewing me, wanting to know what I thought of Venetian people and gondoliers (I liked all I had met), where I lived in California (San Jose), how old I was (31), what other languages I spoke (a little Spanish), and if I was writing this project as a student (nope). We got sidetracked for quite some time while I realized how necessary it was for them to trust their interviewer. I also took this opportunity to shoot some photos, the sleepy gondolier still hiding behind his sunglasses and continuing to snooze and Giannino hamming it up and exaggerating his poses. Stefano let me try on his hat and had me pose on the back of his gondola with the oar in my hand. I felt ready to topple right into the canal, especially since I was wearing my favorite Florentine heels, and made them promise to fish me out.

But soon, again, I was the outsider as a conversation between Giannino and the older man grew louder and more animated, stealing everyone's attention. I finally asked Max what was going on, and he explained that there was to be a boat race that Sunday, a practice run for September's Regata Storica. The prize was 25 million lire plus bonuses from local papers and wealthy families.

"Are you going to be in this race, Max?" I asked.

"No, no," he smiled back. "This is not for the regular gondoliers; it is for the people who train for it, hours every day," he explained. Only one or two regular gondoliers were racers, such as Paolo D'Este.

I grabbed my pad of paper again and pumped Max and Stefano for details. The Regata Storica contests had four categories: the caorlina, involving six standing men in a long boat; the mascarette for a team of two women; and the puparino for young men under eighteen. Lastly came the most-watched gondolino, where two men rowed a smaller gondola using greater technique than strength. Sunday's race, however, was for racing gondolas. The course wound around Murano, an island in the northern lagoon, and the men debated over exactly how many kilometers it covered.

"If you come to the Fondamente Nuove on Sunday," offered Max, "you can see it from there."

Any pretense of an actual interview degenerated completely after this. Giannino, who I had had to hold at bay with a stick the previous year, kissed my hand and pouted with his woebegone eyes. He was a tall hunk of a man with close-shaved hair and large, round eyes, not showing much family resemblance to Stefano who, while also tall, had a slighter build. Giannino reminded me of a gladiator trying to masquerade as a teddy bear. The previous summer he had offered me a "free" gondola ride then spent an hour trying to convince me to kiss him for good luck under every bridge. Just then, tourists came to hire him for an hour's gondola ride, letting me off the hook. I hesitated in rebuffing the men's flirtations too forcefully; in the interests of future interviews, I wanted to keep on the good side of them. And frankly, since I had had a boyfriend for some time, I wasn't used to fending off advances. I felt caught up in my excitement at starting my project, but also caught between being nice and not being taken advantage of. While I found my balance, in the meantime Max teased the napping gondolier about not paying up for ice cream after losing a card game. Paolo pointed out that Condom, at age nineteen, was Venice's youngest gondolier (eighteen being the legal age for a license). The older man pulled at his eyebrows to show how he came by the nickname of Diavolo, meaning devil. And the gondoliers took their turns ferrying the traghetto in a daily, day-long dance on this turn of the Grand Canal, drawing disappearing swirls like invisible ink on an unfurled scroll.

Giorgio, also known as Diavolo, was nicknamed for his pointy eyebrows.

Stefano with his charming smile.

Gramoe

"I walk in a spilled taut quality of motion, an
architecture of light."
--Harold Brodkey on Venice

"If you like, I show you my house and you see my wife," Stefano offered as he stepped onto the pier. I had just finished shooting a few photos of the covered gondolas docked at San Felice, hoping to capture their melancholy aloneness, when I recognized Stefano as he arrived to moor his boat for the night. I had pointed the camera at him, but he had barely paused, anxious to get his boat covered before the rain began. Two porticos faced the Grand Canal in this picturesque spot, a former traghetto stop with a dilapidated wooden dock and a couple of fat white columns holding up a three story orange apartment building.

As the daylight had faded, I had hurried outside with my camera, hoping to capture some images before losing the light—or before the storm arrived, promised in thick, blue-gray clouds. The evening light was gorgeous, causing the colors of Venice to seem to glow from the inside: tawny orange, eggshell white plaster, and burnt sepia tones. More than Germany's austere cleanliness, I loved Venice's crumbling beauty, the plaster walls that seemed to perennially flake away, revealing layers of color, or the algae that crept up the sides of walls or under bridges. Frequently, I wanted to run my palm across walls wherever I walked, to test the dense textures. I was constantly enraptured with the romantic images surrounding me as I strolled the city. At the same time, a salty, swampy smell floated on the light breeze.

When he finished putting away his equipment, Stefano and I then walked together along the wide shopping street of the Strada Nova to the Santa Sofia traghetto stop. His walk was fast and business-like, and he leaned his body forward as if this would propel him faster.

At the traghetto, Stefano changed from his gondolier attire—black slacks and a red and white-striped shirt---to street clothes. Through the open door of the casotto, I accidentally caught him in the act of changing into shorts, his boxers showing. "If you don't mind?" he said, smiling and raising his eyebrows. "I mean, I don't mind, but I don't have a very good body," he apologized, holding his stomach.

Why was he changing in open view of me? Did the men always do this, or was this another form of flirtation? I decided to play along and pretend to be "one of the guys," as if, as the serious journalist I was hoping to be, I wouldn't be fazed by this locker room display. Keeping it casual, I reassured him about his tummy, "You have nothing to worry about." Stefano, like most gondoliers, was lithe and strong. It took great upper body strength to row boats all day long and athletic legs for balancing while poised on the back of the boat. From being in the sun all day in summer, gondoliers are tan and hearty. Stefano put on a beige Ralph Lauren Polo shirt; "I wear the Polo," he said. He was mad for these, elated on the day he discovered that he could order them online. Since these shirts were cheaper in the States than in Italy, I became his Polo supplier on subsequent visits.

Once we started heading toward his house, I asked

Stefano what his "gondolier" name was, his nickname, or sopranome. Virtually every gondolier was given a sopranome by his colleagues, denoting some trait about him. He looked over my pad of paper to check my spelling as I wrote "Gramoe." "And what does it mean?" I asked.

"It is this," he replied, puffing out his cheeks like a squirrel and touching the rosy patches. "There is no translation for this word," he explained. I was still mystified. Maybe it was some sort of reference to his being Giannino's younger brother, the cheeky boy with the innocent face. But did an innocent personality follow? As I got to know him better, I found that it did not. He could swear with the best of them, teaching me many foul words, and telling gossipy, lewd stories about his comrades.

We walked quickly through the streets since the dark clouds still loomed overhead, now blotting out the fading sunlight. Stefano led me through the back streets rather than the main thoroughfares. After a day of working with tourists and being around so many people, he liked the silence and emptiness of back alleys, he explained. Many of these alleys were no wider than the two of us as we strode side by side (and I resisted the urge to run my fingertips along the plaster). The tall apartments blocked out most light, so we walked in shadow. Stefano took rights and lefts with determination. We passed right by the apartment I had rented, which I pointed out to him. "Oh, this place? I think this lady is crazy," he commented quite accurately about my landlady.

I mentioned that I liked the rain and hoped it would start soon. "Yes, but it is a problem, you see," he explained. "For me, there is not so much work when it rains." Even though the idea of the acqua alta, the flooding water, seemed picturesque and even fantastic to me, Stefano explained that it was very dangerous. "When the high water alarm sounds," he explained, "the people who live on the ground floor have to move all their furniture. Many things get damaged."

Stefano ranked practicality above all things romantic. I also asked about the snow. "There are maybe two days of snow each year," he told me, "but it's very bad, especially for the old people. The water turns to ice, and it is very dangerous. The old people do not go outside." Something that sounded so fascinating or attractive to a visitor was, unfortunately, a big problem for the people who had to actually endure it as a part of life.

We strolled on through the Santi Apostoli parish toward Fondamente Nuove at the northern edge of the island. The area consisted mostly of tall apartments and a few businesses, particularly marble carvers since we were nearing the cemetery island. In the enclosure of a campiello, or small square, Stefano rapped on a window to summon his wife to open the front door for us.

Stefano's wife, Michela, was petite and pretty and had her short dark hair lightened to match her husband's. She worked as a secretary for one of the wholesalers near the Piazza San Marco. Stefano had told me earlier that he and his wife wanted to learn more English, but she was apparently too shy to practice with a foreigner. She didn't say much to me, asking Stefano to translate for her. I got to peek in at their sleeping seven-month-old baby girl Sara and had a short tour of their few rooms and kitchen. Good apartments were a scarcity in Venice, they complained. Their place was thoroughly remodeled on the inside, with a modern kitchen and white-tiled bath; I was particularly impressed with the heated white towel rack attached to the wall, drying towels quickly, while at my apartment all I had was a clothesline outside the window where I lived in fear of pigeon droppings. "This building," Stefano explained, "it is from the thirteen century." He appeared unimpressed. Nothing in my homeland could compare, yet this was his everyday dwelling.

With glasses of Coke Light in our hands, Stefano

showed me his personal computer, which he used primarily to improve his English. He also proudly pulled out a couple books in English that he had acquired when tourists had left them behind at the traghetto. Nabokov's *Speak, Memory* seemed like a daunting task for someone with limited proficiency. He explained, "I sit with the book in one hand and a dictionary in the other, and I read that way."

Stefano didn't get to spend as much time with his new daughter as he would have liked. The summer months were the busiest time for gondoliers, and they usually worked ten to twelve hour days or more, trying to earn enough for the lean winter months. With his cheerful disposition, Stefano shrugged away the long hours because he knew it was necessary. At the end of each day, Michela usually met him at Santa Sofia with Sara in her stroller. The two sets of grandparents, all native Venetians, babysat during the day.

I came to realize that Stefano and Michela were a sort of dying breed. They both were born and grew up in Venice and continued to live there, not on the mainland like so many of their generation. They still spoke dialect at home, and though they spoke it to their daughter, she would only hear Italian at school. Venetian dialect might be lost by her generation. Stefano's thirteenth century building, his language, his profession, his historical legacy, all were handed down to him as a sort of bequest, yet these were all things he took for granted. At the thought of their loss, or the inevitable decline and sinking of his city, Stefano merely shrugged. "I don't care. I will be gone by then," he said. He lacked a single sentimental bone in his body.

The next day would be Sunday, the day of the big boat race. Stefano suggested that I stand on the main bridge on the island of Murano. From there, I would see the finish of the race, the most exciting part. His brother Giannino had a motorboat and they, their friends, and wives were planning to attend the regatta. I secretly wished to be invited but certainly didn't feel comfortable enough to invite myself along.

With the rain finally pattering tentatively down, Stefano walked me out the door and down one narrow street, pointing out the way to Fondamente Nuove, the long promenade facing the northern lagoon. From there I'd be able to find my way home. Some gondoliers, I mused, were just regular men wanting to provide a nice life for their families, not at all like the stereotype of the super-macho Italian lover. Stefano had expressed a wish to someday move to California, but he explained with his characteristic shrug, "I have a singular kind of job. I cannot do this there." I exchanged kisses on the cheek with both him and Michela as I left, happy to embrace this Italian custom and pleased with myself that I was getting to know some real Venetians.

Two gondolas docked and covered at San Felice.

Paolo D'Este takes a long lead in the Murano regatta.

An Exhibition of Strength and Fearlessness

Despite weather reports forecasting more rain, Sunday proved to be a beautiful day. In the afternoon, I caught the vaporetto—the Venetians' word for ferry—to Murano, the island of the glass factories. Smaller than Venice, it consisted mainly of two wide canals with fondamenti, or walkways, lining them. Virtually every shop along the way sold glass, for Murano is the island famed through history for its skilled glassmaking. In fact, glassmakers were given special privileges in the past just so they wouldn't leave their island and share their secrets with others. Following Stefano's advice, I made my way past the colorful buildings and slow shoppers and found myself at the large black iron bridge facing the Canale Ponte Longo at six o'clock to see the boat race, where I had a great vantage point. My timing was nearly perfect. I had gotten there early enough to pick a prime spot but not so early that I had a long wait. Where I had disembarked at Murano's southeast corner, I had seen the colorful gondole preparing to start the race, while dozens of boats of every description ranged nearby. Soon I would see the racers round the corner, about a quarter mile in front of me. Already, people in their motorboats were scooting into positions, lining the wide canal to watch the race.

The word "regata" evolved from "riga," the wide canal where the races were held. Boat races have a long history in this maritime republic, from the "Feast of the Marias" in 1315 to the Regata Storica held on the first Sunday every September. Surprisingly, the regatte weren't started for their entertainment value; instead, the Arsenale shipyard needed a constant supply of skilled rowers for the many boats it produced. Consequently, competitions were created to keep the men in shape and as "exhibitions of strength and fearlessness."

This race was a preliminary to the Regata Storica in September, which drew hundreds of thousands of spectators every year. Nevertheless, it was a much-watched event for the locals and especially for the gondoliers who understood the technique necessary to row the gondolino. Rowing in the races requires more technique than strength; it's a matter of balance and facility with the oar, pushing it precisely through the water. The rowers wore a standard costume of white slacks, a blue and white striped shirt, and a white bandanna tied around their foreheads. Though most wore deck shoes, I noticed that one man had taken off his left shoe, the foot with which he pushed his weight forward.

The boats were painted bright colors to signify their numbers: 1-white, 2-yellow, 3-violet, 4-light blue, 5-red, 6-green, 7-orange, 8-pink, and 9-brown. The bold hues reminded me of houses on the island of Burano, similarly painted as to be easily identified by drunken fishermen at the end of the day. Racers would start from a pontoon in the lagoon near Murano's first vaporetto stop, travel through a wide canal for half a mile, continue under the iron bridge I stood on to a turning point, and race back again under the bridge to finish before a judges' stand.

Waiting for the first gondola racers to appear from around the bend, I noticed the many types of boats lining the wide canal—yachts, rowboats, wooden boats and metal boats and fiberglass ones. Countless styles of motorboats zoomed swiftly down the canal before tying up along its sides. Every Venetian owns a boat, and I could see from the baked on suntans that many of these folks spent lots of time taking full advantage of their vessels. Local residents continued to ascend the bridge where I stood until all the railings were lined two deep. I listened, uncomprehending, to the rapid and vociferous conversations around me, always punctuated with enough hand gestures to whip up a meringue.

Suddenly, a band situated along the right side of the canal struck up a march as the first rower turned the corner and came into view, and the onlookers burst into shouts and applause. Boat number 8, the pink one, was in the lead, and it was a lengthy one. The gondolier rowed steadily with a strong stroke, while most of his adversaries broke form more often. This was the legendary Paolo D'Este. He leaned his weight forward with each push of the oar, looking like he might tip forward into his boat. His sleeveless t-shirt displayed his massive arms, and his six and a half feet of height seemed to dwarf the gondola. His reach was long, the oar's flat blade thrusting gallons of water behind him before he fluidly maneuvered the oar, blade now parallel to the boat, back to its starting position. He rowed with the same precision as the mechanical statues of Moors who ring the bell in the Piazza San Marco.

An announcer rattled off the placement of the contestants as if they were horses on a track, and the excitement of the crowd grew steadily. One old man next to me tapped my arm and smiled, expressing his enthusiasm for the race. Feeling linguistically lazy, I merely smiled as if I comprehended his Italian. As the gondolas flew under the bridge where we stood, the onlookers skipped quickly to the opposite railing to watch their continued efforts. D'Este was easy to keep an eye on in that pink boat but also because of the thick ponytail hanging down his back. I leaned over the edge of the bridge to shoot photos as each racer sped by, pink in a vast lead, then three more in a pack, followed later by another three, and two men in the rear. These last two certainly didn't look like they were enjoying themselves, though the audience cheered them as heartily as the first.

Paolo D'Este had maintained a five boat-length lead and easily took first place, the others trailing in to the finish line. I learned later that D'Este always placed first. Unlike most of the racers, he was a professional gondolier, daily working at the San Marco station, the most prestigious one. Other gondoliers always spoke his name with admiration and a certain proprietary pride, as he was one of their own. He was always "Paolo D'Este," as if enunciating his full name evinced greatness or maybe simply to pay homage to the long line of minor royalty from which he descended. His stance certainly bespoke majesty.

As the placement of each contestant was announced over a loudspeaker, the boats drifted slowly before the judging stand. Then I noticed that a small white fiberglass motorboat near that stand held four of the gondoliers I knew from Santa Sofia, including Max and Giannino. I had first spotted Max's sculpted black hair as well as his sculpted physique, then recognized the very tall Giannino beside him. They stood in the tiny boat, beer bottles in hand as if they were poised at a bar instead of balanced in a boat. It struck me as odd to see them in civilian dress--tank tops, light colored slacks or shorts, the ubiquitous shades. With the race's end, Giannino turned the boat and scooted quickly under the bridge where I stood, their wake trailing like a comma. Max turned just in time to see me wave, so I blew them kisses like an actress greeting her fans.

The Fraglia

I had been warned: there is little time to talk with most gondoliers because they were "crazy for the money," in Stefano's words, during the tourist season. Why should they relax and make small talk when customers could be cajoled into taking rides? After all, even though the gondoliers of Santa Sofia knew how to have great fun at their work, the traghetto was still a business, with boats to row, equipment to maintain—and even a bit of bureaucracy to maneuver. Knowing every moment was a precious money-making opportunity for a gondolier, I was grateful to be able to tag along with Max and Stefano on their afternoon rides with customers or as they worked the traghetto boats. This sort of "free gondola ride" I was lucky to accept fairly regularly.

"Come, you ask me questions now," urged Stefano with a wave of his hand. He and a partner were to man the traghetto for this half hour, and Stefano took the stern of the boat, which required the brunt of the rowing to propel it. Stefano had me sit on the worn boards at his feet while he worked, and I squinted into the afternoon sun to direct my questions to him. The other rower, who spoke little English, smiled warmly in welcome. This man was probably near Max's age, his early 30s, a little stockier and a little less handsome than the others, with a dark-haired wife who met him at the traghetto at the end of each day.

Earlier in the day, I had walked out to the Squero di San Trovaso at the southern end of Venice, the oldest existing shop still producing gondolas. Within its two wooden barns, or teza, I had seen boats in each stage of creation, from cutting and fitting the boards together to painting the final black coat or sottomarino. The barns opened onto a sloping dirt yard, where boats could be rolled down to a small canal. Three or four men worked at hammering, nailing, and painting half a dozen gondolas perched on sawhorses. I smelled sawdust mixed with salt air. Next to the squero and before an expansive campo stood the creamy white church of San Trovaso. I had ventured into its gloomy interior to see the altar built to secure the health of all boatmakers. The carved redwood-colored marble showed an old-fashioned gondola with both ends curved up towards the sky.

Curious about these vessels, I asked Stefano about his gondola, and he was happy to answer that he had bought a new one just six months before. He had paid 30 million lire for it (about $20,000) and received six million when selling the old one. The great advantage, he explained, was not in its shiny new looks. "When the gondola is older," he said, "it is much heavier because it takes on a lot of water. An older gondola weighs maybe 20 kilos more, so it goes much slower. It is more work for the gondolier," he added with a shrug and a wry smile. Stefano was pragmatic and approached his career as a small business owner. While honoring tradition, he didn't want to make more work for himself, either. He had already tried a career as a Murano glassblower, but the intense heat and assembly-line art didn't hold his interest for very long before he followed in his brother's footsteps, choosing to become a gondolier.

We had already crossed the Grand Canal a couple of times in the traghetto. Stefano had to pause in his explanations to call out directions to his partner at the other end of the boat: "Wait for a boat," "Row quickly," "Let this person on." Directing his attention to me again, he continued, "For example, a gondolier takes maybe fifteen minutes to row from San Marco to Piazzale Roma in a new boat."

I was impressed (and a bit incredulous). "That's very fast."

"Yes," he smiled in answer, "but with an older gondola, it takes an hour." Even with his exaggerations, I could see why he was so pleased to have his new boat.

"How often do you have to repaint your boat?" I asked, thinking of the young sandy-haired man I had seen at the squero carefully applying a shiny lacquer-like finish to an upturned gondola hull.

Looking down at me from the raised rear end of the boat, Stefano answered, "Usually two times a year." Then glancing at the date on his watch, he said, "I have an appointment in September to have my boat painted. It needs it right now, but this is the time when I can make the money." He also told me of the especially hot summer two years before that damaged the boats more quickly. I was beginning to understand why gondoliers kept heavy tarps on their boats and turned over the cushions when they didn't have passengers, protecting the fabric from the harsh sun.

I pressed further, asking how long it took to paint the gondola. With this conversation I was feeling more like a successful journalist, gathering information even if my methods were casual. "It takes about two weeks," replied Stefano, and explained that autumn fogs or rain would slow down the work. If the weather was good, he said, the painter might even finish in one week. During that time, Stefano could try to borrow a boat from another gondolier, maybe someone on vacation; they helped out each other in that way.

Stefano then pointed to the stone foundations of the Pescheria, the fish market facing Santa Sofia that our traghetto was approaching again. "You cannot see it right now," he said, pulling a frown, "but in January and February at low tide, you can see the damage where the waves have cut away at the stone." Even with a speed limit of five kilometers per hour on the Grand Canal, which few boats actually held to, the motorboats and vaporetto did considerable damage. While air pollution ate at the buildings above ground, it was the advent of motorboats that would truly be the death of the city's foundations.

Out on the water, the slight breeze brought some relief from the humid and stifling summer heat. Stefano had rolled up the cuffs of his black slacks to try to cool off. I had noticed others often doing the same thing. Stefano had previosly complained that the president of the gondoliers' association had decreed that the men could only wear black slacks, not white ones or, heaven forbid, shorts. When working the traghetto, most men wore simply the black slacks and a white shirt, sans the straw hat, rather than a more colorful striped shirt.

Remembering this conversation, I asked Stefano about this president. "Do you vote for him? Is it like a union?" I inquired.

"No, no," he was quick to say, "It's not a union. Last year, the gondoliers worked for a company, and we had to pay them so many lire. But they never do anything," he said, scowling. "They just want our money for doing no work."

"And this year?" I asked.

"This year, every gondolier works for himself. It's much better," he said, constantly rowing and maneuvering the traghetto while we talked. He rocked forward, pushing against the oar with power from his legs. It seemed that each gondolier, as I got to know him, displayed a particular subtle style of rowing, from how he held the oar to how he walked the two steps to reposition for rowing. Stefano looked like he rowed without thinking, as natural as striding down the street. On the other hand, Max stood solidly and with a commanding presence; in fact, when I later saw the film *Wings of the Dove*, which both of them acted in as gondoliers, I could pick out Max by his stance alone since the shots always cut off the gondoliers' heads.

"But what about this president?" I prodded, returning to our topic. "Did the gondoliers vote for him?"

"Yes, but he doesn't do anything," Stefano repeated. "We each pay him 50,000 lire [about $35] for the year." Showing that this was a subject that angered him, Stefano went on to describe a new program this president wanted that, however, did not hold with the gondoliers. The president wanted to institute a traghetto pass for tourists, charging them 1,000 lire per crossing. Venetians, on the other hand, would cross for free. Though Stefano liked the idea of doing something nice for the Venetian people, who he worked with the most, he knew it would bring in much less money for gondoliers working the traghetto. Many apprentices, in fact, already made very little money working the traghetto as they prepared for the gondolier exam. Obviously, the gondoliers were not pleased with this president. Though gondoliers had formed a brotherhood, or fraglia, these associations were loosely formed alliances of mutual help, not tightly run organizations. I was rapidly forming a picture of gondoliers as a breed of their own, a rather cliquish society of men used to making their own hours and having their own way.

I had lost count of how many times our traghetto had traversed the Grand Canal with its full loads of locals and tourists, the old and young, people with bags of groceries, and even baby carriages. Most people stood during the brief crossing, but some of the older women had squeezed onto the board next to me until I was squeezed out onto the well-worn boat's narrow side board. Spotting his wife Michela with baby Sara in her carriage, Stefano said, "This is my last time today." The other gondolier proffered his arm to help me off the boat, while Stefano disappeared into the casotto to count out his share of the day's earnings. I felt grateful for this insider's glimpse into the workings of the gondolier's profession, one that had not been disclosed in any text. It was a free gondola ride of a sort, nothing glamorous, but certainly enlightening. Next, I hoped to meet more members of this brotherhood to see if they would be as friendly as Stefano or, as I had been warned, if they would refuse to share their world with me.

A gondola being scraped and painted at San Trovaso.

The Pescheria, a fish market facing Santa Sofia.

Mario glides down the canal, hamming for the camera.

Rescued by Cappuccino

I could feel the water slogging around in my shoes and looked down to see that my rain-drenched dress had created a growing puddle on the white tiled floor. Mario looked down, pointed and laughed and said something in Italian to the worried waiter in his bright white caffé. I wondered how to say "I'm sorry" in Italian, but just laughed along with Mario and sipped my cappuccino instead.

While having a glass of wine earlier at my local favorite, the tiny Bar Lucciola, I had heard some distant rumbling and hoped it might bring some rain. The water in the canals was looking very low and was starting to smell fishy and pissy. Within fifteen minutes, as I sipped my Barboso slowly, the afternoon sky had grown dark, and a fierce wind whipped the wrappers and cigarette butts from the sidewalk into a frenzy. My practical side urged me to get my camera to my dry apartment before the rain began in earnest, but instead I relished strolling slowly down the middle of the now-deserted street. Within twenty steps, however, the rain went from scattered drops to a drizzle. Gondoliers on the canals I passed rowed to port furiously or scrambled to cover their boats. Within another twenty steps, the rain became a downpour. Lightning flashed and thunder boomed. In ten more steps it had become a true cloudburst.

I giggled and smiled to myself crazily, getting big eyed stares from the people huddled herd-like in the storefronts and caffés as if they were afraid of melting. I walked up to the Santa Sofia traghetto stop, thinking that the trellis would provide a cover from which to watch the rain fill the Grand Canal. Wind whipped the darkened canal into little peaks and splocked against the lacquered boat sides. Water poured into the canal so rapidly that I felt I could watch its level rise. The rain poured down so furiously that my dress became plastered to me. I was beyond hope, yet I felt energized by the carpe diem ridiculousness of it all. I waved off offers of refuge from gondoliers holed up in the casotto because I recognized the one curly-headed blonde who Stefano had warned me was so stupid. "Him," Stefano had nodded his head and rolled his eyes some days before, "he is like this," he finished, rapping on the stone wall beside him.

As I stood there, a fire boat came roaring down the Grand Canal, all the firefighters standing huddled at the prow like toy Weebles in their orange coats. A fire in this downpour? After ten minutes with no slowdown and the wind becoming steadily chillier, my practical side finally did get the better of me and I decided it was time to seek shelter. However, within five steps, bean-sized hail engulfed me, chunking me on the head until I ran, laughing, to the welcoming gestures of the gondoliers and waiters at the corner caffé. When Mario called out "Cappuccino," I gave in to sanity. Mario braced a muscled arm against the doorframe and stretched forth his other hand like someone pulling me from a swollen river.

That's how I found myself creating a puddle on their

poor floor.

The waitress put down some rags for me to stand on, and Mario bent down to wring out my dress. I leaned an elbow against the black marble bar as I scraped the hair away from my face. Another waiter brought me a white towel, which I used to dry my face and arms. I noticed Mario's compact build and rough hands with large calluses developed between his thumb and forefinger, just where an oar would rub, I supposed. When my coffee arrived, he insisted that the barista sprinkle chocolate on top. He twisted his gold ring off his finger to show it to me, a ring formed by two pali, the striped poles where boats tie up, with a fero placed between them. It was a copy of his grandfather's ring.

"And your father, was he a gondolier?" I asked. "And your grandfather?"

"Sí," he replied, turning down the corners of his mouth. "And before him, his father, and his father, and his father." He raised his fingers higher to form a ladder into his past, then called for the waiter to bring me another towel. A woman wearing far too much makeup peered at us over the rim of her cup. Mario's English was quite limited, and at that time my Italian was non-existent, but we managed to have a conversation by employing pantomime where language left off. Max had earlier told me that Venetian dialect is closer to Spanish than Italian, so occasionally I dusted off my high school Spanish and tried substituting Spanish phrases in order to be understood.

Next, Mario pointed a thick finger at the fero on the ring and counted to six, first in Italian and then in English. This fero had only five prongs representing the sestieri and the sixth for Giudecca.

"Why are there only five sestieri?" I asked.

"It was different in the past," he pointed out. "Dorsoduro and Giudecca were one, only Giudecca." His hands formed a whole island. "Then it changed: Dorsoduro," his hands separated the parts, "and Giudecca," he finished.

"When did this change?"

"Oh, maybe in 700, 800."

How does one reply to such a daunting timeline? Later, I delved into some history on the fero and found out that it became more ornamental in the 16th century, though feri had between three and nine prongs then. By the end of the 16th century, the feri became more consistent, and the prow fero generally had six prongs. The stern fero remained similar to that of the prow for quite some time before shrinking in size and ornamentation. "So how long have you been a gondolier?" I asked Mario next.

Mario's eyes twinkled under his long lashes, so thick they almost made him appear to be wearing mascara. "Too long," he said, smiling. "No, it is 21 years." Then he pointed to some of the other gondoliers who had come inside for drinks to warm them. Pointing to a sun-weathered man who looked maybe 45, Mario's age, Mario told me that he was 60. The man next to him, who had a brush of white whiskers running under his jawline like an Old Man of the Sea, Mario said was 70. "He's been a gondolier for 60 years," said the mischievous Mario. I didn't believe a word of it. The others, overhearing Mario's words, had their own comments, which I didn't understand, and some supplementary hand gestures, which I did.

"So, are your sons now gondoliers?" I asked, draining the dregs of my cappuccino and finally feeling a little drier and warmer.

"Sí," he replied, and told me, mostly in gestures and bits of English sprinkled with Spanish, how he had been separated from his sons and their mother for ten years. When the sons came to visit, they asked dad for money and then spent a lot of time with their friends. But Mario's warm smile betrayed the pride and love he felt for them. Apparently, he had raised them to be gondoliers, riding in the boat with him, learning to clean and care for it, and so on. But the sons were young, a teen and a twenty-something, and weren't ready to settle into a profession yet. They lived with their mother on the mainland. As we chatted, the group of gondoliers and waiters in the doorway pretended to chant an American Indian rain dance, as if the downpour weren't already enough of a blessing.

Since Mario worked at the Santa Sofia traghetto, I asked him if he knew Max and some of the other gondoliers I had met. I had to use Max's gondolier nickname, "Campagna," for Mario to know whom I referred to.

Again came a "Sí, sí." Calling for a fresh drink for himself, Mario explained how there were maybe 60 gondoliers who worked out of Santa Sofia, rotating from day to day. Groups of ten to fifteen would usually stick together, working the traghetto, then splitting up to work a nearby canal, then Santa Maria Formosa church, then a bridge near San Marco, and so on. His hands formed little groups that hopped to the next station in a circle. The would-be Indians in the doorway started chanting again and stamping their feet.

Mario worked in a different group than Max and Stefano, though I knew I'd run into him again as I traversed the Grand Canal on the traghetto. Perhaps because we had shared this caffé refuge, a cappuccino, and some conversation this day, my money became worthless to Mario in the future. He never let me pay for the traghetto again and instead always sent me on my way with a kiss on each cheek. Usually expecting equality back home and paying for my fair share of everything, I decided it was nice for a change to be treated to a free crossing or a cup of coffee. It made him happy to give me this small gift, and what did it cost me? I didn't feel any less equal as a person, certainly. In fact, I felt rather special. And who was I kidding? I knew the special attention had something to do with my sundresses and willingness to chat, unlike many Venetian women who kept their distance from gondoliers. But despite my book project, I was also on vacation—maybe also a vacation from my usual self. Traveling allows one to adopt a new persona for a time, like trying on a new jacket.

The hail had finally stopped, the rain slowed somewhat, and the cold was giving me goose bumps. I thanked Mario for saving me with a warming cappuccino and shook that strong, callused hand before venturing back to my dry apartment for clothes that didn't squish when I walked, reflecting on the situations I was finding myself in as I met another member of this group of men.

Sudden Storm

a dimming sky
impetuous wind in the alleys
in a flash
drenched through
long dress stuck to me like
it was poured on
water skating over my lips
in their smile

others huddle in doorways
wide eyed and stunned
a helpless herd on a hillside

choppy canal waters
peak in surging waves
and slap on boatsides
with a splock
gondolas bounce and prance
in their pali

puddles collect in my shoes
I spit the drips off my lips
and laugh
imagining happy tadpoles
between my toes

Franco wears his signature green-ribboned hat.

Double Happiness

One of my Venetian pastimes was wandering the winding alleys for hours actually trying to get lost. After my first few days in the city, though, I had developed an instinct for the labyrinth and usually couldn't lose my way. I soon learned the word corte (courtyard), which often signaled a dead end. The previous year, I had sought out many an alley in the Castello district, east of San Marco, my favorite being one where a silvery canal fish often leaped into the air, startling me as I sat silently reading.

On a particular morning, before many of the tourists had risen for the day, I visited a bookstore just behind Basilica San Marco, where I found a poster showing the many varieties of Venetian boats. The air conditioning in the store almost fooled me into thinking it held the morning cool until I emerged into the blazing Piazza San Marco. Then I wandered east, stopping at the bridge over the Rio del Vin for a look at the gondolas lined up there to see if I recognized any of them. Though the gondolas were uniformly black, they differed in the color of their cushions and floorboards and tarps, in their lanterns, flowers, or flags on the prow, and in the rugs or tapeo on the stern where the gondolier stands. The portela a spigalo, a wooden board that slides over the storage space in the prow of the gondola, differed on each boat, becoming a signature piece to distinguish each gondola. Max's boat, for example, featured a painting of two masked revelers at Carnevale.

As I studied the line of gondolas below, I heard a "Hello" from the gondolier beside me. He was a man around my age with very clear eyes, a strong jawline, and an easy smile. He was the only gondolier I had seen with a green ribbon on his hat. As he lolled casually against the bridge's black iron railing, I noticed that he used a purple bandanna for a belt.

"Hello," I replied. "How did you know I was American?"

"I didn't," he answered. "You look more like the English. Besides, most people speak English."

After he queried me about my country, Franco introduced himself and asked me why I was in Venice. Should I divulge that I was writing about him and his kind? I didn't sense that Franco was a wolfish type, preying on a woman traveling alone like many men did, and I didn't want to scare off a potential friend. After all, I was here to talk to gondoliers—men—so I walked a tightrope between putting up with their advances and gathering information. Might I also make more friends?

"Venice is a very inspirational city," Franco continued with just a glimpse of a smile. He had a relaxed confidence about him, not evidenced by a assertiveness but by an inner calm. "Are you a painter?" he asked.

"No, I am here to write," I answered, deciding to be vague, a little protective of myself until I knew him better, especially since he didn't come with an introduction like the men at Santa Sofia. When he asked what I was writing, I told him that I hoped to write articles for magazines and maybe a book (which I was feeling a bit vague about myself after my initial haphazard interviews at Santa Sofia). I changed the subject, taking the focus off me, asking Franco if he enjoyed being a gondolier. A steady stream of people strolled by us over the bridge.

"Yes, I can work as much as I want," he said. He effortlessly pulled himself up to sit on the wrought iron railing of the bridge, perching as comfortably as any piazza pigeon. "Now I try to save my money to buy a house."

Stefano had told me a few days before that houses in Venice were prohibitively expensive. Franco agreed. "Yes, but then I will have more stability. This job is not very stable," he said, gesturing with his hands to show a flat earth. "Then I can travel." He went on to tell me about his trips to Alaska and New York, where he spent a month walking around the city. When his friend there suggested he take the subway so he could explore further, Franco said that he could see everything just by walking.

"The Venetians walk all the time," he explained. "This is very nice,' he emphasized, "so the people meet each other in the street and talk every day. They are not in their cars." It was true, and this arrangement made it easier for me to meet gondoliers to interview as well. "It is said that every hundred meters there is a bridge. So all day, the people walk up and down." His fingers walked in demonstration. "The Venetian people have the lowest percentage of heart attacks," he added. That made perfect sense, for I was feeling healthier myself every day, and I could feel the difference as my legs became stronger.

I noticed Franco's gold pendant, a Chinese character I recognized, and had to ask about it. "Isn't that the Chinese symbol for marriage?" Most gondoliers I had met sported gold chains as thick as my pinkie, usually with crosses dangling from them, so I was intrigued by Franco's choice.

"It means great happiness," he explained. "I wear it for that. I am not married."

"Yes," I replied, "it stands for double happiness. It looks like two people joined together, so it is also a symbol for marriage."

After fifteen minutes of this kind of small talk, which continued innocuously, I decided that I'd better move on. I didn't want to appear too eager, thinking of the advice from Stefano that most Italian men would see me as a single woman, not a serious writer. Besides, I didn't want to be a vulture, swooping in to ask a bunch of personal questions of a stranger, then flying off again. I'd rather make some friends and develop some trust.

It would be nice to be friends with some of my "subjects" and not be anxious about them hitting on me. All week I'd been sipping at this cocktail of adventure and flirtation, with a dash of homesickness and a twist of nervousness tossed in, as I set about my interviewing task. But in this brief meeting I was fashioning a picture of Franco as quite independent and adventurous, not merely a casanova seeing how far he could get, but a person with more layers to explore. I was curious to know more about his travels, yet afraid of coming on too strong or keeping him from his work. Traghetto workers have breaks between their shifts, but the men working a particular bridge need to reel in customers like big fish if they want to make any money that day. Still, something about Franco told me that I'd see him again, especially if I continued my walks around the city.

"I will be right here all day," said Franco as he waved to say goodbye. I strode away, returning to the labyrinth.

The Red Cucumber

Max was just coming in from a sweltering stint on the Santa Sofia traghetto while another gondolier took his place. He was wearing my favorite shirt, a sort of ripe mango color, under a white boater's jacket.

"Ciao," Max greeted me. "Today is a good day for the visit. Later we have the anguria."

"What is that?" I asked.

"It is the vegetable," he said, looking at a loss for words. Max shaped his hands into an elongated sphere. "You know, it is green outside, like the red cucumber." I wasn't so sure I wanted this mystery vegetable, but I figured I'd stay around to try it—at least out of curiosity.

On a hot, clear day in Venice, the streets empty out. Locals flock to the beaches at the Lido, and only a few tourists venture forth for a gondola ride in the sweltering heat of the day. With nothing else to do, the gondoliers are left to while away their time. But the Santa Sofia gondoliers, I'd found, were masters of enjoying life—whether it be with good food, flirtation, or the occasional card game. Even a hot day at the traghetto was a celebration of life.

I'd known the gondoliers of Santa Sofia just long enough to know that the mystery food was not the only pleasant treat they held up their sleeves. And curiosity had yielded some wonderful surprises for me many times before, such as trying squid ink pasta or discovering a hidden cool spot. So perhaps it was natural that I'd been drawn here to them, to endure the hot afternoon with some company. I'd just spent a couple of air-conditioned hours in the Ca' Rezzonico museum, then remained in its cool entryway licking tiny spoonfuls of vanilla ice cream and writing postcards until the woman guarding the front door began to eye me suspiciously.

Having worn out my welcome there, I'd crossed the Grand Canal on the San Barnaba traghetto with two sullen and taciturn gondoliers—no joking or shouting directions around there! (Small wonder it was a less-used ferry than the fun-loving Santa Sofia route.) With a painful blister starting to grow on my foot and my only other option to go home and stare at the ceiling of my apartment, I bought a bottle of prosecco as an offering and headed to the Santa Sofia traghetto.

I found the usual gang present and accounted for: Max, Giannino, Stefano, others I knew, and a few I hadn't been introduced to yet. There was one nicknamed Neptune. "The King of the Sea," he called out proudly. The men pointed to young Condom, who chimed in for himself "The King of the Bed!" Today, he was the napping one, making me wonder if his nickname had anything to do with his tiredness.

After Max had greeted me with his cryptic promise of the "red cucumber," he pulled up a chair to the white plastic table, and out came the deck of cards. Max and Giannino began another of their rapid, interminable, and mystifying games of madrasso, a complicated, traditional Venetian game. Some of the cards had kings and queens on them, like the face cards I knew. But there was nothing resembling a club, spade, heart, or diamond. The two of them leaned forward in their chairs, focused on the flying cards, forgetting about work.

Stefano and I sat at one end of the white plastic table and stared languidly at the cards as the players flipped them over and scooped them up rapidly. As I watched, the game seemed to resemble hearts, where the player to lay down the card of highest value got to pick up the bunch. Sometimes, one of the men threw down then snatched up the cards so quickly that no one could possibly see what card it was. Every time I thought I was starting to catch on, I realized I was totally lost again.

"I have watched this game for three years," confided Stefano, shaking his head, "and still I don't understand it. It is very difficult, this game."

Giannino, who often lost, wanted to kiss my hand for luck. Max kept score, rapidly totaling columns of numbers in black felt pen in the margins of a newspaper. He claimed I must be good luck for him instead.

I pulled out the bottle of prosecco and plunked it onto the table, then offered some chocolate as well. Every European I know loves chocolate. However, these guys all turned down the offer, grabbing their little bellies and claiming they were fat. They all looked trimmer than most American men I knew. Stefano pinched his little love handles and said that in the summer, with the long work hours, he never had time for the "body gym."

"But I have some small weights at home," he explained and demonstrated how he tried to build his arm muscles.

"Doesn't rowing the gondola all day give you big muscles?" I asked.

"No," he said, frowning. "When I row, I never feel it." Later that evening as I was reading a book I had bought about gondolas, I understood why this statement made sense. In his book *The Gondola: An Extraordinary Naval Architecture*, Carlo Donatello wrote that the gondola's build and the Venetian style of rowing were so well engineered that propelling the boat really didn't take much effort, just a lot of learned skill.

The never-ending card game eventually did end, and Giannino looked smug for having won. Usually, Max was the victor. Apparently, the game required a good memory; Max could remember which cards had been played and which were still in his opponents' hands. When Max left to do a stint rowing the traghetto, Stefano gossiped that Max gambled often, and for big stakes, at the local casino. "Sometimes he loses two, three million lire," Stefano said, while Giannino nodded. Max never betrayed an ounce of stress over anything; gambling was a game, gondoliering was a job, women were a pleasure. None of it was worth any worry.

It was too hot a day for many of the tourists to want rides through the bright and torpid canals. The men hung their heads, looking for something to do. Stefano's brother Giannino, who spoke little English, grabbed the felt pen and wrote "I love you" on the newspaper, pushing it towards me. When I reminded him that I had a boyfriend back home, he asked, "You no have friend for me?" looking dejected. I drew a heart with an arrow through it, and Giannino added a jagged crack down its middle. Beneath his first words he wrote, "I kiss you."

At this point, Stefano impatiently took the pen from his brother, wanting to see if his English was correct. "I want to kiss you because I fall in love," he wrote, and I added, "With you" to the end, thinking to make this into a proper English lesson instead of a flirtation, or to keep it on the level of a game. Then he whispered to me, "All them are jealousy because you have the boyfriend. They all want to try with you."

"But you are a gentleman," I told him, hoping he'd take this as a hint. I was trying to deflect the conversation and keep it lighthearted and fun.

"No," he said curtly and added, "all the gondoliers, they just want to fuck."

Max interrupted this conversation by sauntering over and sitting on my lap with his crotch practically in my face. I threw my hands up and looked at the others, rolling my eyes. "Isn't your lover coming to town soon?" I asked him, trying to distract him. Max had a "permanent" girlfriend as well as a couple long time lovers. He complained that his girlfriend was a bit heavy, but when I met her later I disagreed. She looked like she wouldn't need to worry about dumping Max and replacing him with a more faithful man. His Roman lover turned out to be a gorgeous brunette, perfectly proportioned, well dressed, open, and friendly.

But Max took my hint, apparently, and got off my lap, though only to instead stand behind me and start massaging my shoulders. "What's in here?" he soon asked as he undid the top button on the back of my dress in order to see what kind of bra I was wearing. "It is white," he said, smiling his approval. The other men watched this, curiously silent. All are "jealousy?" I wondered. Their boldness was a bit shocking to one used to lawsuit-wary American men, more cognizant of harassment statutes. But the truth was that it was also thrilling, and my ego was enjoying everything I got. My American boyfriend hadn't been giving me this kind of attention for a while; after eleven years things had worn thin. Giannino liked to repeat, "He is not here. He does not see." Besides, I knew I'd be getting on a plane to go home, never to run into these guys and their expectations later, so why not enjoy the attention now?

Giannino talked rapidly to Stefano (well, all Italian

still sounded rapid to me) and made prongs with his index finger and pinkie. "Cornuto," said Stefano, turning to me. "What do you call these horns?"

"Cuckold," I said and wrote it on the newspaper, realizing that it did sound a bit like cornuto. "When a married woman takes a lover, isn't it called a 'cavalier servente'?" I asked, having read about Lord Byron's relationship with the Venetian Countess Guiccioli. Apparently the cavalier servente was a common institution in past Italian culture. Since most marriages were arranged, not with love in mind but with an eye towards wealth and social standing, many wives took lovers. The man a lady was more in love with was her cicisbeo or cavalier servente who escorted her to social events, carried her fan and waited on her every whim. Had Giannino brought this up because he hoped to cuckold my boyfriend? That certainly wasn't a boundary I'd cross.

"We call it casanova," spoke up Stefano. "There are many gondoliers who work the long hours, so their wives take on a lover."

"And the husbands know this?" I asked, skeptical.

"Yes, yes. It is normal," he shrugged and pulled down the corners of his mouth.

"But don't the gondoliers, the men, have lovers?" I queried with surprise.

"No, they are too busy working."

This blew to pieces all the known stereotypes of the gondoliers as Don Juans, casanovas, seducers, and romantic lovers. I was amazed that these proud men allowed their wives to keep a man on the side. However, I was also incredulous; I had heard enough gossip to doubt this claim. Were they trying to garner my sympathy? Or just pulling my leg? Giannino pointed out that his wife lived just down the street, so she would see if he were with a woman. "No one will have me," he sighed forlornly.

The talk of famous lovers reminded me of something

Max had said a few days before. He was ferrying a Swiss couple through the canals, conversing in German with them, and he had invited me to sit on the stern of his gondola while he rowed. Occasionally, I would understand some of what he told them as he pointed out famous sites, one being Casanova's house out near the Fondamente Nuove. Just the day before, I had overheard two other gondoliers pointing out Casanova's house in the San Marco district on the other side of town. With a suspicious tone, I asked the men where the real house of Casanova was.

Paolo took the map and explained with a sly smile that Casanova's house was anywhere the gondolier wanted it to be. "If the tourist rides around this area," he drew a circle with his finger near San Marco, "then they see Casanova's house. If they row around here," he continued, indicating the area near the car park, "there is Casanova's house. The tourist wants to see these places," finished Paolo with a shrug. I could always count on him for a straight answer and a clear explanation. Paolo's comment was confirmed by the others.

Stefano piped up and said, "Casanova was in many houses because he had many lovers."

"But I want to know where Casanova's house really is," I insisted. Paolo and another man conferred and dotted my map on the Rio di Santa Marina. Later, my research turned up more possibilities, houses where Casanova was born, lived, had affairs, so in a way, they could all be right.

My reading on Casanova also included a few volumes of his huge memoirs. He had had hundreds of lovers and cuckolded many husbands. Each woman was a conquest for him, yet at the same time he truly loved many of them. Love, to him, was not the "till death do us part" contract as so many defined it; instead, it was a pure appreciation of the woman for her beauty, and yes, even her mind. He lived in the moment and couldn't commit beyond it, but his love burned sincerely. Contemptible and immoral as many found his behavior, after reading enough to realize that this was Casanova's attitude, I found I admired his freedom to love and to not be ruled by social custom. His viewpoint seemed to be shared by many of his modern-day namesakes.

As four o'clock came round, the men sent Condom, the youngest gondolier present and therefore the gopher, to fetch a knife. When he returned, Paolo set to work slicing up two cantaloupes while they, Stefano, and I stood to eat the slices with our fingers, leaning forward and dripping juice all over our hands and the ground. They called it simply melone, so I described our many kinds of melons available in California: honeydew, Crenshaw, casaba, and others more exotic. When we finished, Stefano turned the table on its side and hosed everything down.

This was repeated a little later when Giannino arrived. Max had said they were bringing the anguria, a "red cucumber," and I wondered what kind of vegetable that could be. Giannino opened the brown paper bag to reveal a gigantic striped watermelon, which was then carved and handed round as more of the gondoliers came up to the table. Max grabbed each piece as quickly as he could and ate the heart first while Paolo tried vainly to shoo him away. They ate the seeds, too, instead of spitting them out as I was used to doing. Juice patterned the cobblestones. Plastic cups appeared and the prosecco was opened with a pop and poured, though many of the men abstained.

I had been there for over three hours, and, besides the traghetto work, these men had had few tourists come by requesting gondola rides. "The other gondoliers," explained Stefano with a look of disdain, "they don't do this, eat the snacks at four o'clock." He indicated the melon rinds and juice that Paolo hosed away. "They only want to make the money, not spend it on food. They don't know how to enjoy the life."

Traghetto Santa Sofia

suntanned gondolieri
you give a girl the shivers
practicing English by writing
I love you
I kiss you
and discussing the cuckold's horns
all are jealousy
him and him and him and me you say
Giannino, Diego, Paolo, Stefano
names to make my mouth round and musical
the boats wait unloved
while pink melon drips from our lips
and juice on our hands and the stones
washing off with the hose
and swallowing cupfuls of prosecco
a broken heart drawn on the newspaper
all gondolieri without lovers
hard to believe

Max, also known as Campagna, looks for customers.

Il Casanova Moderno

"Dice a Campagna," Mimo enunciated slowly in Spanish so I would be sure to understand, "'morti cani.' Es una palabra que todo los venezianos conozcan." I repeated the phrase to him a couple of times to make sure I had it right, but I figured that if it was a word all Venetians knew, Max would be able to understand this message from Mimo.

I had just crossed the Grand Canal at Santa Maria del Giglio by traghetto, oared by Mimo and his partner. They had noticed the book I carried, *El Gondolero y su Gondola* by Eugenio Vittoria, given to me by Max that morning as I set out to visit the Accademia Museum. Max had gotten the book from the gondolier company he worked for, but he could only find the Spanish translation to give me. Luckily, I read enough Spanish to understand a good portion of it, but the book contained such interesting and valuable information that I wished I could buy an English translation for myself. Best of all, it turned out that the book had opened the door to meeting another gondolier. We stood in the sun-baked, narrow square before a bright orange wall that reflected more heat. The nearby boathouse was nearly walled in behind thick ivy. Few other gondoliers appeared to be on duty, unless they were hiding indoors.

Mimo and his colleague had thumbed through the book in the boat before they ferried me across. The sun was high overhead, so Mimo's little chestnut-colored mutt Chicco, who rode along in the traghetto, had crawled under the wooden seat to find some shade. In fact, due to the heat, Mimo wore only a white tanktop, an indiscretion he could be fined 300,000 lire for (about $200). No matter the temperature, gondoliers were required to wear black slacks and shirts with sleeves, or any police officer had the right to fine them—though of course, if the offending gondolier was a personal friend of the officer, this result was unlikely, and gondoliers were pretty friendly fellows. Mimo's deep tan looked good against his white tanktop, and his stocky frame showed that he had taken good care of himself for his 45 years. He always wore his shaded glasses and usually had a curved brown pipe clamped between his teeth, even when he was rowing.

On the way back to my cooler apartment, I stopped by Santa Sofia to deliver Mimo's message. "Max," I said to him where he sat in the shade with Stefano, Giannino, and the usual crowd, "I met Mimo and he said to tell you 'morti cani.'" With this the men all howled with laughter and slapped their thighs or stood up to laugh harder. "But what does it mean?" I cried out.

"It is better you do not know," said Max, laughing and showing his large white teeth. None of them would reveal the phrase's meaning to me, but I could guess that it must be pretty foul.

"Next time you see Mimo," Max told me, "tell him that Campagna says, 'figlio di mamma troia,'" and with that all the men broke up again. Here, my small knowledge of

Spanish and Latin allowed me to translate "figlio" as "son," and from there I could safely assume the rest. I was being used as a messenger for profanity.

Friendly and familiar to people all over town, Max said "Ciao" numerous times as he strutted in his jaunty way whenever he took a break from work to have lunch or get a drink. He played soccer every Friday night with friends while juggling a girlfriend, a long-time lover, and any short-term relationships passing through town. Any gondolier I asked knew who Campagna was, despite the fact that he lived outside Venice. I had even seen him momentarily moor his gondola full of paying customers so he could make a phone call, probably arranging a tryst.

One evening as I sat outside a caffé on the Strada Nova, Max was passing by with his confident yet casual swagger, and he stopped to help me drink my carafe of red wine. Silver metal tables were closely arranged before the caffé's large, green, wooden shutters. I kept having to scoot my chair aside as others came and left. He was wearing a chartreuse shirt embroidered with the word "Rugby," which would have looked hideous on anyone without a tan as deep as his. As usual, a pair of pricey sunglasses was perched atop his head. He told me how he had just bought these because his others had fallen into the canal that day. "If you look at the bottom of the canal, you see all the sunglasses of Massimo," he said with a laugh.

Max chatted a bit first with the barista and then with the waiter, men who had been hospitable towards me earlier. It was another rainy evening, so the waiter helped us move our things to a table under the green awning. After working all day, Max was hungry and insisted that I join him for a snack. Soon the waiter brought us sandwiches of red and yellow roasted peppers, slippery between their toasted bread. Max knew I was living in Venice on a tight budget, and he seemed to want always to feed me, giving me bites of his panino and treating me to drinks any time I stopped by the traghetto to say hello. "What do you eat in your room?" he asked, knowing that I usually couldn't afford to eat out.

"Well, I eat bread and fruit and cheese," I said. "The signora across the hallway sometimes brings me coffee or breadsticks." I suppose I sounded pretty down and out.

"You eat just the bread?" asked Max, raising his eyebrows, "nothing on it?"

"I like Nutella," I replied, mentioning that chocolatey spread.

Max sat up quickly from his slouch, looking astonished. "Nooo," he cried, breaking into a smile. "I love the Nutella. Every day, I eat the big jar," he said, indicating its size with his large hands. "Sometimes I get the pimple."

Scores of people streamed by on the Strada Nova, the "new street" that used to be a canal. Still animated, Max told me that his lover was returning from a trip to Rome. I had met her the previous year; Max must like long relationships, despite his many brief encounters, because he had kept this lover for some years and yet also had kept the same girlfriend for eight. Though his girlfriend knew this other woman, she never suspected that Max was unfaithful to her (or maybe she chose not to acknowledge his infidelities). Perhaps any woman who had snagged this handsome, charming man would be willing to look askance at his amorous adventures in order to keep him. Max was the quintessential Casanova. Apparently managing to convince countless women to surrender to him, Max sincerely loved them—at least for the moment or a few days or weeks—like Casanova had. And the women ate it up, one after another. Max possessed that charm, that philosophy, and that luck.

"The man and the woman, they are different," he asserted. "Women love more with the heart, but men love more with the body," he said, leaning forward. I conceded that this was true of many men, though not all, because I knew a few of the exceptions. Max thought I was probably deceived in this belief. Max continued to explain his thoughts. "I don't like to make love only the one time and say goodbye," he said. "For me, I like to have the relationship with the woman and be the friend, too." This statement contradicted what some of the other gondoliers had told me about Max entertaining a string of women as they vacationed briefly in Venice; I had heard that Max was used to spending only a couple of days with a woman and that he often tired of one if she stayed in the city longer. But I wanted to give my friend the benefit of the doubt.

However, I knew first hand that Max could understand a "No." The previous summer when I had first met him, he had tried to add me to his list of conquests. But when I assured him that I was faithful to my boyfriend back home, Max stopped pressuring me and remained my friend. This year when I arrived in Venice, he joked, "Now I have two wives and three lovers," counting on his fingers. When I told him I still had my same boyfriend, Max said, "It's okay. I no want a lover." Why should he? He already had enough women in his life.

When the rain slowed and the wine ran out, Max paid the bill and we walked back around the corner to Santa Sofia. Darkness had descended and the crowded street had thinned. There we stood to admire the lights reflected on the canal, creating orange and white ribbons on the black water. "Since it rained all evening, how will you explain to your girlfriend why you got home so late from work? I wouldn't want you to get in trouble because of me," I teased. I felt safe flirting with him. I had a long history of telling him "No," so I think he believed it by now.

"It's no problem," he replied. "My girlfriend, she always wait for me and cook me the nice dinner." I felt a bit sorry for her, knowing the whole truth about Max. We parted and Max strode off down the Strada Nova with his cocky gait to retrieve his car at the car park for the short drive home.

I found out much later that Max had married this girlfriend two months before. And in true Casanova fashion, he had spent the entire night before the wedding with another woman, one who was in the wedding party. I wasn't so much shocked as amused; Max's actions didn't match my morals, but he didn't surprise me, either. The title of Casanova fit him, just like that bright rugby shirt, but so did the Venetian nickname for a teller of tales—Pinocchio.

A Different Breed

The rain seemed to be my lucky charm—and Venice was having an unseasonably rainy summer. I had left visiting some American friends who were spending a few days in Venice and set off to stretch my legs after the hour-long boat trip from Burano, one of the nearby islands in the northern part of the lagoon. The sky was looking darker by the minute, but I didn't pay it much attention; last week's storm and the one the day before had both been wilder, colder, and longer than normal, so I didn't expect this one to amount to much.

I guessed wrong. Just as I crossed the large bridge behind the Bridge of Sighs, I felt the first raindrops. But as luck would have it, just at that moment I also spotted Rico, a gondolier I had met the previous summer. Rico, young and thin, was lighter complexioned than many of the gondoliers I knew. He spoke English with a British accent, Italian being his second language. Though he could be disdainful when talking about his colleagues, he was always spritely and amiable with customers, often showing an impish smile. He had the swagger of the unproven teenager about him. I ducked under the awning where Rico stood to wait out the rain with him and chat. "This rain isn't about to stop," Rico said, peering from under the awning at the dark sky. "Let's go down the street to the bar to wait." Once there, we slid into cold metal chairs at an outside table, tight against the wall and under a small awning where the rain splashed up onto my legs and a chunk of white plaster dropped from somewhere above me, like careless carpenters from the heavens were at work.

Neither the money grubbing entrepreneur, nor the carefree spendthrift, Rico was a different breed of gondolier. He maintained a faithful honesty with his customers as well as a healthy cynicism towards his fellow gondoliers. However, he also recounted the gossip and dirt on some of the gondoliers I knew, telling me who had lovers or conquests, who lied, and who cheated the tourists. He disclosed how one of the gondoliers I knew sometimes exposed himself in public, displaying his prodigious talents. "One time two of the guys were playing football—you know, soccer—in the square by the traghetto," Rico said, "and the game got a little rough. They started to wrestle, and your friend pinned the other guy to the ground, sitting on his chest. Then he undid his pants and pulled out his dick and waved it in the other guy's face." Rico told the story with great glee laced with a hint of admonishment and distaste, though I couldn't tell if that was for my amusement or his own.

Next Rico revealed that another of the men was the perpetrator of the "free gondola ride" story he had told me the previous year. A hippie girl in a long skirt, smelling of patchouli, had walked up to the Santa Sofia traghetto asking how much a ride cost. "For you, it is free," the gondoliers chimed. One gondolier then took the woman on a "free" twenty-minute ride, returning to the gondoliers' applause as he approached the traghetto. "Free" gondola rides were always paid for, even though the currency might not be lire. It was this story that I kept in mind each time I was offered a ride.

I saw Rico as sincere and trustworthy, but also I didn't want to believe some of these people that I had become friends with were capable of such deceit or vulgarity. Perhaps I was too naïve or trusting (the first time someone told me that gullible wasn't in the dictionary, I actually picked it up and started to check). Then again, Rico was known by the gondoliers as "Americano," attributed to a childhood residence and also to his status as an outsider. Gondoliers are a very cliquish bunch. They didn't seem to trust him, nor he them. What game was being played? And by whom?

Rico complained about the money-conscious crop of tourists he had seen this year. Most of them cajoled him for discounts. When I inquired about the pricing, wondering if gondoliers haggled or set their own prices, he said that the rate was set and had to be posted at the gondola station. "There has been almost a fifty percent price increase in the last year," he exclaimed. "The gondoliers are pricing themselves out of business." In 1996, a fifty-minute ride had been 80,000 lire (about $60), and now it cost 120,000 (about $80). At night, the price rose to 150,000 ($100). With obvious contempt, Rico revealed that many gondoliers cheated their customers by not clearly stating the price at the outset and then taking them on the Grand Tour, which cost extra. He admitted that only once had he treated a customer less than fairly; when the man had been extremely rude to him, Rico took him on a shorter tour, but by rowing very slowly, still stretched it out to fifty minutes. Yet as I got to know Rico better, I heard his stories of convincing tourists to take the "Grand Tour," which wasn't so grand, or I heard his expectations of big tips, especially from Asian tourists. He might not be cheating his customers, but he still was out to get what he could.

Switching topics, Rico asked if I still had the same boyfriend as the previous year, to which I nodded. He wondered disdainfully how the casanovas at Santa Sofia had treated me. I described my gondola ride with Giannino the previous year where he had turned into an octopus with lips after rounding the first corner. But I told Rico that I did have to defend Max who, after a few firm "no's," realized I meant it and remained respectful. "You make it sound like all the gondoliers are unfaithful lechers," I said, a bit protective of those I counted as friends.

"No, there are some decent chaps," he relented. "My brother is a good man and is absolutely faithful. Then again, his wife is stunning and can think; he has no reason to be unfaithful." Rico continued to name a couple other trustworthy gondoliers he knew. I began to wonder what he might say about me when I wasn't present.

And what about Rico's love life? He described two women he had cared for the most. One was an American from West Virginia who was a born-again Christian and wouldn't dream of leaving home and joining Rico in Venice. The other was a Colombian woman living in Los Angeles who twice spent a number of months with him. "But I don't know if I'll ever find the right girl to marry," he said doubtfully. "Here in Venice, I meet only the tourists. And the Venetian girls, well," he plucked at his striped gondolier t-shirt, "they see this and keep going." He asserted that, unlike most gondoliers who wanted merely a cook and a maid, he wanted a wife with a brain, a will, and a personality.

The previous year, Rico had worked as an apprentice at the Santa Sofia traghetto stop, where I had first met him. As an apprentice, he was often mistreated, pushed into taking others' shifts and occasionally not paid his share. But Rico was smart and had the perfect key to open the door to his gondolier career: family ties. His brother, his father, and many generations farther back had all been gondoliers and, in fact, Rico's eventual inheritance included his father's gondolier license to work the San Marco region, a much-coveted and lucrative position. Gondolier licenses were for a certain station or area, and they were priced according to the money-making potential of the location. Rico knew he only had to bide his time as an apprentice; he had already easily passed the licensing test the previous fall. He had his own gondola but was still licensed as a substitute, probably until his father retired and ceded him the permanent license.

Rico revealed his dream to me. "I'll probably work as a gondolier for six or seven years and save my money, then return to England to university," he said. "I passed my A level exams, but a bad thing happened at that time. Margaret Thatcher cut off all aid to students." Rico's mother was from England, which explained his accent, and he had spent a good portion of his life there, including much of his childhood and his education. He sometimes advertised himself to prospective customers as the only native English-speaking gondolier in Venice, though I realized later that his brother could claim the same title. He added as an aside, "God knows I don't need that sort of education to be a gondolier. My father started working as one at age thirteen and he's been a great success."

"So what do you plan to study and do with this education?" I asked. I was beginning to be chilled by the rain falling just inches from me, but the downpour was too steady for me to head home in it. Besides, Rico was easy to talk to.

Lifting his chin a bit, he replied, "I want to sit on European parliament." I was a bit surprised, not imagining that he had such lofty aspirations. But he explained that he was in the ideal position to run for one of the seats. "I have citizenship in two European countries," he explained, meaning Italy and England, "and actually, I was born on a small island in the Caribbean, so that's on my passport, too."

Rico explained that only thirty percent of the eligible European population voted for the Parliament, so it wouldn't take many votes overall to secure a seat.

Since Rico's English was impeccable, I decided to check a few of my facts with him. I told him of the book I had recently bought, *The Gondola: An Extraordinary Naval Architecture* by Carlo Donatelli, which analyzed in detail the gondolier's rowing technique, power of thrust, and so on. Donatelli even delved into laws of physics, leaving my understanding quite murky. Though I had thought that rowing required strong arms, Donatelli wrote otherwise. "Is it true," I asked Rico, "that rowing a gondola doesn't take all that much upper body strength?"

"Yes, it's all right here, actually," he replied, slapping his right thigh. "You push with this leg and lean into the oar." Rico also mentioned Paolo D'Este, the San Marco gondolier who won the regatta I had seen at Murano. "He's huge," said Rico, holding his arms up and apart to illustrate a set of wide shoulders. "Not that he needs to be. It's in the technique, too."

We had been sitting at an outside table this whole time, and now the rain was beginning to worsen dramatically. It started blowing in on us sideways, and the wind became very cold, forcing us to move inside. "This must be a storm straight off the mountains," Rico said incredulously. We were like two people stranded on an island—him, unable to work and me, unable to get home without freezing and getting drenched. We moved to an indoor booth with a modern Formica table. Air conditioning buzzed and pretended to cool the swampy air, while the rain continued to pour steadily into the alley outside our window. Tables were green, walls were green, waiters wore green aprons in this, the Bar Verde.

Soon the thunder and lightning set in right overhead. Rico was becoming concerned about the gondola he was using. His own gondola was moored across town, and he had borrowed one near San Marco so he could get an early start on the day. There had been another rainstorm the previous night, and Rico explained, "A lot of tourists have their hearts set on a gondola ride, and if they didn't get the chance to do it last night, they'll be out early this morning looking for a gondolier." Now he worried that he would have to shovel water out of both boats. We stepped out of our caffé, dashing from awning to awning, trying to return to the borrowed boat. I was in a summer dress and was growing goose bumps. Rico finally gave in and bought a huge rainbow striped umbrella so we could reach the boat without becoming completely waterlogged.

Through unrelenting rain, we rushed up the street, the cobblestones now slippery. The canal behind San Marco had already risen at least a foot. Steely gray water peaked and crested in the wind. Rico grabbed his backpack off the boat so he could change into a less obvious t-shirt than his striped gondolier one. The continuing downpour made it useless to attend to the boat. Rico then pulled a small pipe from his bag, and we hid inside a wooden construction site barrier, me holding the umbrella overhead so he could smoke a bit of hashish. He said that getting stoned while working was one of the perks of the job. I guessed that he wouldn't be allowed this same privilege when he sat on parliament.

Rico was unsure whether he should quit for the day or still hold out hope that the storm would relent. While we stood indecisively on the nearby bridge, a fellow gondolier came by and told Rico to take care of some business at the gondolier station. Rico walked me back to the Bar Verde to wait out the storm. I soon warmed up with red wine and a black polo shirt lent to me by a waiter. After an hour and a half, which included five chapters of *Anna Karenina* and a basket of potato chips, I gave up waiting for him and started home through the last sprinkles of rain.

But to my surprise, there at his borrowed boat

crouched Rico, bailing out water with a red sessola, a little wooden shovel. "The canal's awfully warm," he said, looking up at me with a sly smile. "It makes me think there's a lot of urine in it." Rico explained that his father had found him and insisted they have dinner together and that he had passed by the caffé twice, unable to get my attention. Uh huh. What was that about? Just then he was approached by a sunburned German father and son inquiring about a gondola ride. "You're here for three more weeks still," confirmed Rico, "so I'm sure I'll see you again. I'll be working out of the San Tomá station; you can find me around there." As friendly and forthright as Rico seemed to be, I was also picking up on some duplicity—he was not the same as many of his colleagues, but also he was not the pillar of morality. A different breed but still a dog.

A bird's eye view as a gondola passes under a bridge.

Andrea, the lean wolf, pauses to say "Ciao."

Il Lovo Uomo

Andrea had quite the charming, broad smile and a gleam to his white teeth.

Every encounter with him lasted no more than five minutes—that is, if I kept them on my terms, not his.

One day, feeling a little lonely and wanting a friend to talk to, I had gone in search of Max. Unable to find him in his usual gondola stations, I started asking other gondoliers if they knew where he was.

"Have you seen Massimo? Donde está Massimo?" I tried in Spanish.

"Which Massimo?" asked various gondoliers.

"Campagna," I replied, thankful that Max had told me his gondolier nickname. But always I received a negative reply. At least having a purpose—searching for a friend—kept me busy instead of brooding.

Stopping at one pretty canal in a busy shopping district, I had queried the youngest gondolier present and the one most likely to speak English. I was intrigued that he wore bright green shoes. But he hadn't seen the elusive Max either, who I later learned had taken off a day to go to the beach.

That evening, I guided a lost American couple, Joe and Louise. I was learning the city, learning its history, and it was fun to share that knowledge. Besides, speaking American English was a nice break from always adjusting my English to simple sentences with no idioms. The couple told me of the charming gondolier they had ridden with that afternoon, a young man who deftly matched up the tourists with gondoliers at his station: the Hotel Splendid Suisse. Then Joe and Louise insisted that we experience Harry's Bar together, and as we strolled through the Mercerie shopping area towards the Piazza San Marco, who should we see but the same gondolier I had spoken to earlier. Louise formally introduced me to him as Andrea, but when she told him that I was writing about gondoliers, he clammed up and shuffled sideways in search of a customer. Scared off that one, I thought.

Weeks later, as I emerged from an alley onto the Strada Nova, I was stopped by a tall, handsome man who inquired, "Remember me? I gave the gondola ride for your parents."

I noticed how lean and thin he was, his cheekbones prominent. He looked starved. It was funny seeing a gondolier not in his gondolier garb. Andrea was one who seemed to always wear his red-ribboned hat, but I was quickly able to place him, especially because he wore his bright green shoes. "But those were not my parents," I explained, "just nice Americans I met who were lost."

"Oh, I'm sorry," he replied, "I not understand because my English is not so good." He told me he had just come from a visit with his parents and was on his way to meet friends for pizza. "But some time, if I see you here, say 10:30 after I work," he said with a wide, bright smile and dark eyes, "maybe we can go for pizza." He gave me a brotherly pinch on the arm, then one on the cheek. Was I really likely to randomly run into him, say, 10:30 after work? What kind of an offer was this? Coupled with his earlier reticence, I was put off.

A few days later, I saw him wiping down his boat after a rainstorm. Won over by my desire to say hello to someone I knew (I spent long hours alone), I stopped to say "Ciao." Andrea's gondola was one of the more opulent ones I had seen, with a rich intagliate or carving on the stern and gilding on the fodra and pusiol along the sides near where the passengers would sit. I could respect the meticulous care he was taking and his pride in his vessel. We stood on the pier under a wooden roof strung with small white bulbs, bright against the darkening sky. At this section of the Grand Canal near the Rialto Bridge, restaurants lined the walkway and cast a rainbow of sparkling lights onto the water: cobalt, crimson, a Christmasy green, reflecting off the faceted lanterns that held them and onto the black water below.

"Where are you going now?" he asked, looking up from his work and flashing those long teeth again. I thought of the Venetian word "lovo," ("lupo" in Italian) meaning wolf, that I had come across just that day in my reading. I told Andrea of my busy day visiting other islands and that I was in bad need of a sweater after the cold storm that had blown in. It was nearing nine o'clock and I hadn't had dinner yet. From the corner of my eye, I spied the full moon glowing brighter in the darkening sky. I still had my camera around my neck after taking a frenzy of photos of the pink and gorgeous sky.

"That is a beautiful camera," he said admiringly. "No," he continued, raising his eyes to mine, "you are beautiful." I stammered a "Grazie," but my palms grew sweaty. Something in my stomach said, "Go!" but trying to be the intrepid journalist, wondering where this story was going, I stayed.

"Day after tomorrow, I make a holiday," Andrea said. "Maybe we meet for pizza?" We talked about where we might meet when we were interrupted by an inquiring customer wanting a gondola ride. Andrea held up one finger and raised his brows, wanting me to wait a minute. Apparently in that minute, his thoughts turned more lascivious. Even with the many people strolling nearby, I felt fear play a minor key. Unlike so many of the gondoliers I had met, I didn't trust this one.

While the prospective customers made up their minds, Andrea stepped off his boat and casually walked over to where I leaned against a column. "I finish work at twelve o'clock," he said. "Why don't you come back for a private gondola ride," he added and placed a hand on my bare arm. Glancing back at the two Asian women wanting a ride, he let his hand slip down to my hip. "You come back at twelve o'clock."

"Let's just have a pizza on Sunday," I said, trying to keep a lighter mood.

"You don't like the gondola ride?" he said, eyes gleaming. "You know how much it costs?"

I thought back to stories I had heard of the so-called "free" gondola rides women had received, rides that were paid for in other ways. "But I hardly know you," I said, stepping back. "How do I know you are a gentleman?" Andrea looked puzzled by the word as if his grasp of English were suddenly failing him. "How do I know I can trust you?"

"You don't like me?" he said with surprise.

"I have a boyfriend." I trotted out my standard line but soon heard the standard reply:

"But your boyfriend not see you in Venice."

I knew it was time to move on. This encounter just didn't feel safe.

"You come back at twelve o'clock?" Andrea prompted me again.

"Maybe. And if I'm not here, when will I see you again?" I asked, testing him.

His reply was a shrug.

My answer was to leave.

Cuckold's Horns

"Cuckold. *n.* A man whose wife has
committed adultery."

All along I had intended to write about the many gondoliers of Venice, not just one or two of them. But it had become easy to hang out at Santa Sofia and chat with the numerous friends I had made there, so I knew I had to push myself to go out in search of new subjects. However, one slow Sunday afternoon about halfway through my trip, I stopped to say hello to the Santa Sofia crowd and caught Stefano in a very talkative mood. Unable to get a word in edgewise, I let him ramble on about the private lives of other gondoliers. Good thing I wasn't a prude because Stefano didn't censor anything. Maybe I was slightly shocked, but mostly I was entertained.

Max was the great casanova, Stefano revealed, though I had already figured this out. While Max unwittingly ferried people on the traghetto just a few feet from us, Stefano and I sat under the trellis in the shade and gossiped about him. He told me of Max's many conquests, an endless list, and like the description afforded the original Casanova, Max sought pleasure with every kind of woman—local, tourist, tall, short, young, old. Since he lived in Mestre on the mainland, Max was able to succeed without getting caught. In Venice, everyone knew everyone else, and they ran into each other on the street or gathered in the campo each evening to share the latest gossip. Stefano was smart to introduce me to his wife right away, or else she surely would have heard malicious gossip about the American woman who talked to her husband so often. But Max lived with his girlfriend—scratch that: wife—on the mainland, away from the rumor mill, and she was blissfully unaware of his reputation.

"Max," Stefano confided one time, "he just likes to fuck. Any woman who goes by—your sister, your mother, your grandmother—he will go with any of them." Stefano made a face. "I think if you put a bag over my head, he would fuck me, too." Stefano pronounced it to rhyme with "quack."

Paolo came and sat with us while there was a lull in customers. Various gondoliers lounged around the table in cheap plastic chairs, playing the ubiquitous madrasso game or sleepily staring at the canal. I almost didn't recognize Paolo with his hair newly cut, nearly shaved off, only black stubble showing his scalp to be pale compared to the rest of him. He and Stefano joked about their wives.

Paolo pointed to Stefano and said, "He just tried to call his wife and she's not home. Then he called to my house."

Stefano interrupted with the punchline. "Maybe they both have the lovers and are out together with them." Paolo laughed while Stefano made cuckold's horns with his index fingers over his ears.

"What is the Italian word for cuckold?" I asked, since I hadn't remembered it from the previous conversation.

"Cornuto," answered Stefano, now waggling his

pinkie and index finger on top of his head.

"That sounds like the ice cream," I replied, referring to a Cornetto, something like a drumstick.

This prompted Stefano to leap from his chair and tell a story simultaneously in English and Italian for the benefit of the other gondoliers present as well as for me. "This old man," he began, pooching out his stomach like a potbelly, "went to the caffé to ask for ice cream. 'Give me a cornuto,' he said," and the men all burst into laughter. "Here in Venice," shrugged Stefano, "it is always a show going on."

About this time, the older gondolier with devilish eyebrows came out of the casotto with another well seasoned gondolier who had a wide gap in his front teeth.

"This one," said Stefano, indicating the gap-toothed man with a thumb, "he is the gondolier who knows everything about the history of Venice." They chatted on, unaware of Stefano's words since they spoke little English. "When the people ride in his gondola, they come away like this," he said, rolling his eyes around and wobbling his head. "He tells them too much information."

Paolo began nodding his head to confirm Stefano's words. "He made a mosaic, too," he added. "It is so good, from one meter away, you think it is a fresco, not a mosaic." I glanced at this man in appreciation.

"He also is a sculptor," Stefano continued. "He made a Bucintoro, maybe one and a half meters across," he said, referring to the doge's magnificent ship of state. "If he sells it, he is a millionaire." With this, Stefano stood up and pantomimed his colleague walking into the bank carrying two huge sacks of money while everyone joined in another good laugh.

I could see past Stefano to the traghetto boat gliding back into Santa Sofia. Some passengers wanted to snap a photo of their friend with Max, who, without prompting, kissed the girl for the picture. There he goes again, I thought.

Glancing at Max, Stefano said, "Massimo's father, he was a great man," and Paolo nodded vigorously.

Paolo added, "With him, there were always jokes and the fun."

Paolo added, "He just retired three months ago. He was seventy years old." I had a hard time picturing a seventy-year-old man rowing a gondola every day, but Stefano confirmed that it was a healthy lifestyle.

"Massimo is like his father," Stefano continued with a knowing nod in Max's direction. "His father had two families," he said and told me of a visit to the father's house. There were no photos of Max on the wall with the other kids' pictures. When Stefano inquired why, the father said, "This is my second family." It was common knowledge in Venice. This wasn't a step- or blended family, like we would call it in America. He simply had kids, plural, with a couple different women.

Dark clouds were scudding in and a cool wind was prickling my legs, so Stefano and I moved our chairs out onto the sunny wooden walkway that led to the boats. Stefano rolled up the sleeves of his red and white striped t-shirt to tan his arms. He told me that there was another regatta that night, this one on the island of Giudecca for two-man gondolas. Paolo D'Este and his partner were expected to win this one as well. With the looks of the sky, though, I guessed it would be postponed.

"Did you see the fireworks last night?" I asked Stefano. I had joined a friendly group of Italian law students from Padua who shared their panini and Tokai wine with me as we watched the fireworks explode over the San Marco basin at midnight. Many people stayed up all night on the Lido beach to watch the sunrise. It had been the Feast of the Redentore, celebrated on the third Saturday in July each year with fireworks in commemoration of the end of the Black

Plague in 1576. A pontoon bridge was erected in a day from the Zattare, the southern edge of Venice's Dorsoduro district, to the Church of the Redentore, or Redeemer, on the long island of Giudecca. In the past, the bridge was built of boats. It was amazing to think this festival had existed for more than 500 years.

"I did not go," said Stefano, to my surprise. "I was tired, and we think the baby would be scared by the noise. It is the first time in over twenty years that I did not go." He seemed pretty unconcerned about missing the festival, which had been the big event on everyone else's mind. I had had a great time with the group I had met, but there was still the part of me that wished I had been invited out on someone's boat, like a true Venetian.

Max carried over a chair and sat down with us for a brief break, saying, "I am swimming in the canal during the fireworks." He paddled his arms in illustration. "I drink too much wine," he added with a laugh. "I am swimming with the bubbles."

Stefano explained that it was very dangerous to be out on a boat in the lagoon during this festival, though even more treacherous to swim in the lagoon, as Max had. "There are so many boats, and people drive over the speed limit to get home quicker," he said with widened eyes. "But who cares if you get home quicker and you have the accident?" He told me of a time when he was seven or eight and his parents had taken him and Giannino out on the lagoon for the fireworks. A bigger boat didn't see them and ran right over their boat. "We thought my father was dead," he said vehemently and confirmed that their boat was badly damaged.

A Dutch couple and their eight-year-old son approached to hire Stefano. After helping them aboard the boat, Stefano invited me to ride along on the back, on the boards behind the cushioned seats at his very feet. I was thrilled; these opportunities didn't come too often, or even if they would all summer, I'd still never tire of them, especially when I trusted my gondolier. If I couldn't be a Venetian noblewoman at the height of La Serenissima, I would take what I could get right now.

Another gondolier gave us a good shove out of the pali. After a short jaunt down the Grand Canal, Stefano turned onto a narrow canal lined with trailing ivy into the heart of the Cannaregio district in northern Venice. He pointed out to his passengers the line of green moss growing along the foundations of the buildings. "This shows where the high tide is," he explained. "Right now is in between, but two times a day there is the high tide, and two times is the low tide." This shady canal was wonderfully cool with calm green water that showed barely a ripple. Few sounds reached us.

As he navigated the canals, Stefano pointed out the more famous homes of Venetian nobles or painters and each church we passed. Many buildings had doors opening onto the water, doors rotted or caving in or hanging from rusted hinges, and stairs slick with algae. Many of the churches' front doors faced the larger canals since people in the past arrived to them by boat. He described the restoration of Santa Maria dei Miracoli and showed us the newest church in Venice, Santa Maria della Fava finished in 1753. Each time we came to a blind turn, Stefano called out "Oeee!" to alert other boats. "This is the horn of the gondola, beep beep!" he told his youngest passenger.

In the Castello district, Stefano pointed out the smallest street in Venice, one that didn't look as wide as my own narrow shoulders. We passed by Mario, the gondolier who had rescued me from the rain and showed me his fero ring, and he called out a friendly "Ciao!"

Soon we were passing under two very low bridges in the area where I had first met Andrea the wolf. I looked up to the walkway to see if "il lovo uomo"—the wolf man—was lurking nearby. Stefano knelt down to pass under the bridge and pointed out the many scratch marks made by the iron fero and popa when the tide was high. I saw crevices gouged into the stone underside of the bridge as I craned my neck backwards. "There was one gondolier that wrecked his boat this way," he said, showing disdain at the man's foolishness. I had recently read that all the bridges were originally flat until the evolving gondola's raised prow and stern necessitated arched bridges to accommodate their height. Stefano moored at the steps of the nearby hotel, where he helped his passengers to disembark. He then rowed us out onto the sunny Grand Canal and back to Santa Sofia.

The afternoon was turning to evening, and my intention of saying a brief hello had turned into a three-hour conversation and gondola ride with Stefano. I thanked him for letting me ride along on the back of the boat.

"It is the same for me," he said, shrugging, "whether you are there or not." Stefano was no flatterer, unlike many of his compatriots.

Putting on an injured tone, with a smile I asked, "Am I such bad company?" But I didn't get an answer from Stefano as he scurried away to help Max's latest customers out of a gondola. It occurred to me that I had once again been the lucky recipient of a free gondola ride, my only payment being friendship. There were exceptions to every rule, and different rules to every game. Stefano trusted me with his gossip and stories, never putting on a false self to get his way. Paolo was the same. It was easy to be their friend.

Full Moon Glide

"Judge the moth by the beauty of its candle."
–Rumi

Despite the fact that Venice has so many places to get lost in—177 canals, 450 bridges, and more than 3,000 small alleys—I inevitably ran into people I knew. This often helped me deal with an itinerant homesickness, that, despite my new Venetian friends, still sometimes assailed me. Though I generally enjoyed being alone, this was my longest solo trip. My boyfriend had chosen to not join me, and I often pondered the many meanings of his choice, for himself, for us, and for me.

One person I ran into with some frequency was Franco. After our initial meeting, I had seen him giving gondola rides three separate times. I'd wave from whatever bridge I was crossing as he glided past with a boatload of tourists, calling to me, "Ciao, bella!" my most favorite of greetings. To be called beautiful so often by so many men was an unfamiliar treat that helped me fight the few bouts of loneliness. I was beginning to refer to this not as my Venice vacation but as my ego trip. Eventually, I came across Franco when he had no customers, sitting on the balustrade of the Ponte de la Canonica, the large bridge just behind the Bridge of Sighs, where hordes of tourists herded past in a constant stampede. Franco was easy to spot in a crowd of gondoliers because of his distinctive green-ribboned hat.

"Did you like the fireworks Saturday night?" he asked. He had seen me on my way to watch them that night. I told him how I had been befriended by a group of Italian law students and had sat on the island of Giudecca.

"I spent the first eighteen years of my life on Giudecca. It is a very quiet place," Franco said. "When I first came here to start working, it was a great shock for me. It was like being dropped on another planet." He mimicked this experience by spreading wide his fingers as if God had suddenly relinquished hold of him. Franco was again living at home with his parents on Giudecca in order to save money. His father, whom I later met, was a spry former gondolier with the brightest blue eyes I had ever seen, and he now spent his days painting scenes of Venice, mostly on the portela a spigolo, the board near the front of the gondola. The family also kept a superb organic garden from which they treated me to dinner. During our conversation, Franco was looking a bit harried by the constant crush of people passing by him all day long, and I noticed how thin he was. As is usual in a conversation with a gondolier at his station, all talk was punctuated by "Gondola, gondola" every few moments as prospective customers trudged past.

Not wanting to interfere with Franco's business at this busy site, I waved "Ciao" and began striding briskly down the street. But moments later I heard running footsteps as Franco caught up with me. "Do you always walk so fast?" he asked, nearly out of breath.

"Would you like to have a drink?" he offered. We stepped into the nearest caffé, the Osteria da Baca, and he ordered glasses of cool white wine. This was a dark, ancient corner bar with wooden tables that seemed to still be coated with residue from their years of elbows and wineglasses. Large, dark brown tiles paved the floor, and a narrow shelf above our heads held bottle after bottle of wine. A group of four older gondoliers strolled in noisily and eyed us sitting together. One of them asked Franco in Italian where his wife and children were, and he translated for me to let me in on the joke. Franco, at age 28, admitted to me that in his younger days he had indulged in brief relationships, but now he found them dissatisfying, almost to the point of being disgusting.

"Did I tell you that I am a doctor of internal medicine?" he asked, almost sheepishly. "That is what I do in the winter time." He explained that, after three years of general anatomy, he was now practicing with the only man in this field in Italy, a field more homeopathic than general medicine. By feeling a person's pulse and body rhythms, Franco could determine which internal organs or systems weren't functioning properly. Usually a change of diet or forms of massage and manipulation solved the problem without the need for medication or surgery. "You would think that in every hospital there would be a person like this. It makes so much sense," he said with some dismay.

Trying to understand this complex field, I mentioned that it showed a lot of common sense to look at the whole patient and not just treat one symptom. It sounded like what many of the ancient Chinese doctors tried to do.

"Here, I'll show you what I can do." Franco took off my watch and placed three fingers along the veins in my right wrist, staring off in space and "listening" with his fingers. He didn't seem to be hearing much and switched to my left wrist. I was a little suspicious, considering the ways gondoliers had "tried" with me before. "There is something with the spleen and the large intestine," he concluded, "but that's all I can say without a complete examination."

It all sounded a bit esoteric, yet it still fascinated me, and I decided to drop my suspicions and just let things roll. We talked a little about alternative medicine and how it wasn't accepted as legitimate by most doctors. Franco glanced at his watch. "I better get back or my friend will be mad," he said, referring to his partner, who was working the bridge with him. We gulped down the last of our wine, and I walked him back to his station. "If you want to go for a gondola ride tonight," he offered, "come back around nine o'clock. I should be done then."

I looked forward to another conversation with Franco, but I was gun-shy about those free gondola rides. I told him the story Rico had related. "You don't have to worry," he said, turning quite serious. "I am not like that." I felt inclined to believe him.

That evening just after nine, I made my way to Franco's bridge, the Ponte de la Canonica. The area was nearly deserted, surprising because it was a beautiful clear evening and the moon was still full. Though I was a bit nervous, my previous encounters with Franco had been promising, and the prospect of a ride under the full moon drew me like a moth to light. I carried with me the American woman's confidence in the word "no" and a fledgling trust in Franco. Besides, I wasn't entirely sure that he would still offer a ride or that I would accept.

I did not see Franco or his partner about, but I did see the legendary Paolo D'Este standing by his boat. This would be the perfect opportunity to approach him since I had a legitimate question.

"Dove stá Franco?" I asked in the few words of Italian I had finally learned, incorrect though they were.

"Franco?" he asked looking puzzled.

"Sí, el gondoliero," I stammered in bastardized Spanish-Italian, "con el verde . . . ," as I waved my hands around my head to indicate a ribbon on a hat.

Luckily, D'Este rescued me from further embarrassment by answering me in English. "He is at dinner. Go down this way," he said, indicating a left turn after the bridge, "and look at the restaurant there, or else look in the next caffé." D'Este was huge, standing more than six feet tall, with a ruddy suntan and long black hair pulled into a ponytail, quite an imposing figure. Standing confidently upright rather than lounging as many gondoliers did, Paolo was much more intimidating than the other men I knew. He wore his straw hat tipped forward on his head, with the elastic strap across the back, under his ponytail.

"Grazie," I said and almost turned to go. It was now or never. After having seen him in action at the race and hearing the awed tones others used when speaking of him, I didn't want to squander this opportunity to get to know this gondolier. "Uh, are you Paolo?" I asked.

"Yes," he answered, looking a little perplexed.

"Paolo D'Este?" I continued.

"Yes. Do I know you?" he asked a bit defensively.

"I saw you in the regatta, the one at Murano," I quickly explained. "You were very fast." D'Este still looked dubious. "My friend Campagna told me who you were," I added, hoping to lend myself credibility. It sure came in handy knowing Max.

"Ah! Campagna, the gondolier," he answered and finally smiled.

Feeling more confident, I asked about the previous night's regatta on Giudecca. I thought it might have been rained out, but D'Este said it was finished before the rain. He and his racing partner had won as expected, so I congratulated him. The conversation came to a screeching halt. I was saved a moment later when D'Este pointed to the green-ribboned hat that had just appeared atop the bridge. But suddenly it turned and ran back the way it had come. I strolled to the bridge to wait.

When Franco returned, he complained about how bad business had been that day. "The time goes by faster when I am busy," he sighed. As we stood there, few people passed, and at times Franco had a despairing look on his face. After one couple refused his salesmanship, Franco turned back to me and sighed, "I really wanted to go with them." I was nearly ready to offer him the 120,000 lire to take me for a ride, but I knew that was a week's worth of food for me.

During the lulls when no one walked by, we continued our previous conversation about alternative medicine and then switched the topic to travel. Franco told me about a trip he had taken to Vietnam that had changed his life. He had felt the wounds that country still harbored and related what a powerful feeling he got from the land and the people. "I felt the coldness of death there," he said fervently. "It made me want to open my heart to the warmth." Instead of talking about the cities he had visited, he went on about the feelings he had experienced. Apparently, Franco had a knack for plugging in to the soul of a place, connecting with its mood rather than merely visiting its sights. He'd go for months at a time, a traveler rather than a tourist, getting to know a place's people and pulse, taking it into his heart. He finished by mentioning the pedicab drivers who he thought were a bit like gondoliers.

"But not as romantic or glamorous," I teased, though I really was feeling impressed by his level of emotions. My trust in him grew.

Franco went on to describe his experience in Israel. "Even though I am not Jewish or Christian, I had this sense that this was a holy place," he said, his eyes burning. "As soon as I stepped off the airplane, I knew something was different. I could feel the years of history there. Important things happened there. It was all around me."

Soon his partner returned with his last group of

customers, and Franco darted down the steps to help them disembark. He obligingly took a picture of the people with their gondolier, then bounded back up the bridge. Full darkness was upon us, and we got little light from the moon beyond the tall gray walls of the doge's palace and prisons on either side of us.

While I sat with his partner on the wide balustrade, Franco tried to engage customers. For three Asian-American women, he climbed up on the stone wall and threatened to leap into the canal if they didn't ride with him. The women giggled behind their hands and kept walking. Another couple with a child refused Franco but then agreed to ride with the next gondolier on the fondamenta, which really annoyed him. He said it must be the moon's influence; since the moon was just beginning to wane, Franco was losing his personal power. I told him to not take it so personally.

Franco and his partner finally looked at their watches, conferred for a moment, then with gleeful yelps jumped for their boats. "Come with me!" called Franco, for they had decided to cut their losses and throw in the towel for the night. Yet the night was far from over. Franco offered a ride, anywhere I wanted to go. I decided that I couldn't live with myself if I refused, spending the rest of my days wondering, "What did I miss?" I might get other offers for free late night rides, but not from a gondolier I trusted as much as Franco.

"What do you want to see?" he asked as he rowed us away toward the northern lagoon, and I settled back against the black cushions, playing with their fringe, giving in and feeling like a spoiled countess.

"I want to see the real Casanova's house," I said, "Or at least one of the many." Even though I had accepted this adventurous ride, I thought I still might learn something at the same time. I guess I hadn't let go completely.

"That could be difficult," he said. "I'm not sure where

it is."

I realized I was acting like a tourist or an employer, and I apologized to Franco that now he had to be rowing—working—even though he had just quit work.

"No, this is different," he reassured me. "Now I can relax." We glided around silently, only an occasional "Oee!" breaking the silence as we neared the blind turns. Though I had walked these parts of the northern district often, they looked very different at night and from the low vantage point of a gondola. Buildings seemed taller and narrower, and canals became elongated. Black sky above and black water below became disconcerting. Silence surrounded us. Just as I was feeling disoriented, we came to a wide canal, and there rose up the buildings of the hospital and the church of Santi Giovanni e Paolo, brightlylit. One more bridge and we'd be in the northern lagoon. The destination became secondary to the evening's beauty.

The night was absolutely silent, no crowds, no motorboats. I began to understand Venice's magic more deeply, what the city must have been like in the past before electric motors. Once onto the open lagoon, the fat waning moon burst out from hiding behind the buildings and flooded the water with a swath of silver light. White seagulls bobbed on the gentle waves, and we coasted away towards San Michele, the cemetery island. We were in illegal waters for a gondola. "The gondola is not allowed here," explained Franco. "It is dangerous if the vaporetto or the motorboat comes because they will not see us." I glanced back at Franco where he stood behind me and wondered if my smile conveyed my joy in this illicit beauty.

I told Franco I had visited San Michele to see the graves of Ezra Pound and Frederick Rolfe, two writers. "My father knew a man who made a bet with his friends," Franco began, "that he could spend the whole night on the island alone. They rowed him up to the wall, and he climbed over," he said, pantomiming the man's actions, "and the man stayed there, getting very scared. Just then, the man felt someone put a hand on his shoulder. It was the caretaker. But the man was so scared that he died of a heart attack."

"Oh no!" I exclaimed. "Is that a true story?" I asked, looking up at Franco with the oar in his hand and the moon on his shoulder.

"Yes, absolutely true," he said.

It was a perfect night for a ghost story, a perfect night for the moon, and a perfect night for a calm glide on the lagoon. "You know," began Franco matter-of-factly, "this year I have not been in the water yet."

"Not even to the beach?" I asked.

"No, I work all the time," he replied. I felt sorry for Franco who couldn't find time to enjoy this place where so many tourists flocked for its sun and beaches and the salty, buoyant Adriatic, who never took time for the red cucumber. "This is a little crazy," he began hesitantly, "but do you want to go swimming?"

How could I do such a thing? That was my first thought. I have a boyfriend. What will people think? Will Franco get the wrong idea? But gazing around myself at the round moon on the glossy, calm waters, I knew I'd regret missing such an opportunity. Carpe diem, I nearly yawped like Walt Whitman, then assented to Franco's request with assurances that all we'd do was swim. When I had set out for Venice with lofty plans to interview gondoliers for a book, I truly never envisioned things taking this turn.

But I am a woman who craves beauty.

Franco rowed us a bit further towards San Michele where the water was only about five feet deep. He turned over his oar and plunged it into the muddy bottom, twisting the blade to rotate it deeper before lashing the boat to this makeshift mooring. Then he turned his back while I stripped down to my underthings and slipped over the side of the boat like a slithery eel. The water was amazingly salty on my lips, like potato chips soaked in brine. It was also chillier than I expected.

I heard Franco splash into the water behind me, so I commented on its saltiness. "Yes, the Adriatic is one of the world's saltiest seas," he told me. "That is why it's so easy to float."

He was right. I paddled around a bit and then stretched down a toe to touch the lagoon's bottom. "It's really slimy!" I exclaimed. "Is it very clean? Are there a lot of fish in here?" Suddenly, I felt alarmed as I looked at the inky water spread around me. What might be swimming beside me? What prehistoric slithery creatures were waiting to suck on my toes or climb inside my underwear? What was living in the ancient ooze?

Franco laughed at my sudden concerns and reassured me, saying, "It's okay here." Being taller than me, Franco could easily stand flat-footed on the bottom. To stay warm, I swam around the boat and up under the prow for a closer inspection. The fero created a fantastic silhouette against the full, pale moon, and it seemed as though its silvery reflection on the water ended at my fingertips. I later had a dream containing this same vision. Gondolas had crept into my very cells.

But the water was too chilly to enjoy this view for long. With my teeth chattering, Franco helped hoist me headfirst back into the gondola, where I landed with a thud and a laugh. He remained in the lagoon while I dried as best I could with an extra shirt and put my skirt and light sweater back on. Once Franco had deftly climbed aboard and donned his slacks and boatshirt, we sat on the floorboards away from the breeze while he rubbed my hands between his to warm them.

"Most people, they never get to see this," Franco confided, indicating the lagoon, the gondola, the moon. I etched the scene into my memory.

I was still shivering, so Franco pulled me closer to him on the cushions, placing pillows behind my back and draping my legs over his. He wrapped his arms around me to warm me up, vigorously rubbing my back and arms. Yes, part of my brain still questioned if I should be there, be sitting like this, allowing this to happen to me. But I couldn't refuse the joy in it, the opportunity this free ride presented. Also, I had always been comfortable with touch, hugging friends often, so this kind of physical intimacy wasn't a big deal. It was my real self, actually, though I still knew where my boundaries were. Soon, the water's chill left me and the night's mild warmth crept back into my skin. We both turned toward the moon and stretched out our legs. "You look like the sculpture," Franco murmured, the moonlight paling my skin. I felt like a goddess.

Glancing at his watch, Franco realized we should head back to San Marco so he could catch the hourly vaporetto home to Giudecca. As much as I enjoyed the moments, I was now relieved that nothing more would or could happen. After pulling up his oar and rinsing off the black ooze, Franco rowed strenuously against the current and the high tide, even having to lean his weight to the left side of the boat at times to give us enough tilt to pass under some of the bridges. He rushed to secure his boat and pull all its covers into place with five minutes to spare. I had met a gentleman gondolier and had been given a gift few ever received.

"Thank you, Franco," I said, looking into those trustworthy eyes, "for sharing this time with me." Where was my journey taking me? Were the shallow waters becoming deeper? Could I continue to balance journalism with friendship—against my needs as a woman?

Midnight Gondola Ride

gliding
in a solemn vessel
on a hushed canal
ebony boat, ebony water
the prow ducks under one final bridge
and oh!
to emerge
onto that glassy black expanse
the moon
wending a silver path
to my fingertips tracing the water's skin
white gulls bob
undisturbed
on gentle undulations
over the side I go
slipping into inky shallows
the saltiness surprising my tongue
and the mud my toes
and me myself
the fero now a silhouette
and I'm under the prow
the lagoon swallows me whole
and the silvery path ends with me

Franco stands at the top of one of Venice's many bridges.

Mimo dons his boatman's shirt for a photo.

Dead Dog

"Campagna dice 'Sei un figlio di mamma troia,'" I repeated from memory. Mimo threw back his head and laughed, enjoying the profane message from Max so much that he invited me to have a drink with him. He clipped the leash onto Chicco, and we strolled to a nearby caffé just over a tiny bridge. The caffé, typical stand-up style, had barely enough room for three people to lean on the glass bar. We squeezed in near the doorway and did a kind of dance as customers constantly shuffled past us.

Hoping to get a complete picture of the territory and a better feel for the gondolier's world, I had decided to devote a day to walking from one traghetto stop to the next. I liked setting myself little goals like this, giving my days shape and meaning and a break from sitting in my dark apartment typing. There are eight traghetti altogether, though there were as many as 43 in 1828. They provide a means for crossing the Grand Canal in the absence of large bridges. Some traghetti are quite busy and may even have two boats in service at once, such as Santa Sofia, while others, such as the lonely San Marcuola, are only open six hours a day and receive so little patronage that the two bored gondoliers nearly fall asleep on the job.

That morning I had begun my trek at Ferrovia, the train station. This crossing was quite near one of the three bridges, but with the train as well as the car park and bus stop nearby, it kept the gondoliers busy. I never did meet any gondoliers there. Next was San Marcuola, where I ran into Giannino with his two young sons and wife just climbing into their motorboat. The boys had sandy brown hair and stared at me, open-mouthed. Except for that departure, the traghetto was as hushed as a graveyard. San Marcuola had a large, spare casotto but nothing else nearby, no trees to fend off the sun, no trellis, tables, or laughter.

I skipped Santa Sofia today since I already knew it so well and continued on to Carbon, just past the Rialto Bridge, where nothing much was happening; Stefano had warned me that these gondoliers were "crazy for the money" and were a "bunch of lecherous wolves." At the next stop, San Tomá, I was ferried across by Rico, who was doing his required stint there. This stop had a small ivy-covered trellis and large locker room in the nearby building for the men to hide from the heat and store their belongings. I peeked inside to see white lockers and long benches, when the stuffy odor of sweaty men hit me. I continued toward the Accademia Bridge to the usually quite dead San Barnaba, but kept on to cross instead at Santa Maria del Giglio. There the ferryman forgot to give me my change from a 1,000 lire note for the 700 lire ride. It was at this stop that I had run into Mimo.

Like the last time I had seen him, Mimo was wearing a white tank top, and he had a bright yellow scarf tied around his neck, striking against his deep tan. While he drained his espresso, he told an acquaintance of the messages I had had the "pleasure" to deliver. Mimo wanted to know the details of Max's reaction to his message of "morti cani," and I told him as best I could. I had grown up with older brothers and a dad who said things like "son of a sea biscuit;" I was used to being around men and being teased, though I had never been duped into using profanity before. Still, it made me feel like an insider, especially because I still experienced a language barrier. Mimo spoke virtually no English, but he generally understood my Spanish and I his Venetian dialect. He confirmed what others had told me—that Venetian was similar enough to Spanish to be comprehensible.

"Where do you stay here in Venice? How long are you here for?" Mimo asked me these questions with seemingly fatherly concern, furrowing his brow. When I told him I wanted to write a book, he expressed enthusiasm for my project. "Good, good," he said, "you are a writer." Though I had published a couple short articles before, I didn't define myself as a writer. But it sure felt good to hear it fall from another's mouth. If he believed it, then I could, too, which I needed since that's what I was here to do. Mimo then told me he didn't especially love being a gondolier, but the money was nice.Like the Santa Sofia gondoliers, he rotated through this station every four days. I practically gulped my glass of soave to keep up with him as we stood through this short encounter. Gondolier breaks were brief!

Strolling back to the traghetto, Mimo saw a flock of pigeons on the wide expanse of stones before us. He told Chicco to sit, unhooked her red leash, then shouted encouragements for her to charge at them. The dog raced across the stones barking, right into the center of the flock, sending them flying. When she returned, Mimo grabbed her rear in both hands and positioned her in front of more pigeons, crying out once again for her to chase them. More short, staccato barks, more startled pigeons. This seemed to be a well practiced game. Passersby stopped in their steady stream to watch this show while others bumped into them from behind.

I asked Mimo if I could take his picture, but first he insisted on donning his white boatman's jacket. "Aspetto," he said and held up one finger as he disappeared into the casotto until he was more suitably dressed. He also made me promise to send him a copy of the photo. Then he made another trip into the casotto where he emerged with a postcard of the Santa Maria del Giglio traghetto. Writing out his address and name, he revealed that his given name was Vincezo; Mimo was a gondolier nickname handed down through the family.

To further his hospitality, Mimo invited me for a visit to some of the other islands. We walked to the edge of the pier where he pointed across the canal. "See there, that yellow motorboat docked in front of the Salute Church? That is my boat." Chatting over a drink and being part of the profanity game were fun—but also very safe. The offer of a private tour put me on my guard. It wasn't a gondola ride, but did it also have a hidden price tag? Mimo consulted his electronic appointment book before telling me to come back on Friday. I decided for the moment to leave this open to possibility but not commit myself to anything. One of my favorite new Italian words was "forse," maybe. "Bring a costume," he advised as he waved me off, puzzled, into the campo. It wasn't till later that I discovered that this meant a swimsuit.

The next day as I crossed the canal at Santa Sofia, I decided to check up on Mimo. Max told me that Mimo had called him to tell of my visit. When I asked Max if Mimo was a man to be trusted—in other words, if Mimo expected more from me than just my company—Max said that he didn't know. "Every man is different," he said with a shrug. "If he tries with you, just tell him you don't want to have sex." That did not sound like fun, especially in my halting

Spanish, and that wasn't a conversation I wanted to have or a position I wanted to put myself in.

I asked Stefano instead because he seemed to always look out for my welfare, and he was always brutally frank.

"Can I trust Mimo if I go with him in his boat tomorrow?"

"No," Stefano replied curtly. "If he asks you this, it is because he wants to try with you." By "try" he obviously meant something more wanton. "Mimo, I think, has children all over the world."

Stefano was probably ensuring my safety with his warning, and I was thankful for it. Max, who was better friends with Mimo, probably didn't understand my concern since he himself was cut from the same cloth as Mimo. Alas, these gondoliers too often lived up to their casanova stereotype after all. Besides, I was there to interview these guys, not date them, right? This line seemed to become blurred with increasing frequency.

"Morti cani," I said under my breath. Though vexed, I took delight in employing my Venetian slang, reciting the phrase whenever I felt frustrated, angry, or incredulous. Things in Venice weren't always what they appeared on the surface, from historical facts to people's intentions. But I guess this applied to me as well. I had intended to write an objective book outlining the history and lifestyle of gondoliers, yet here I was constantly drawn into their lives in ways I didn't always welcome. I didn't want to be in the position to defend or protect myself, yet it came with the territory as I tried to gain trust and finagle my way into my subjects' world. If only someone could take hold of me like Mimo did with Chicco and point me in the right direction, I'd zoom off into my task. As enjoyable as my adventure was, it was no dog's life.

Peste Turistica

Just after six thirty, I appeared at the San Tomá traghetto as Rico was getting off work. Earlier in the day, when I had seen him in passing, he had said that maybe we could have dinner if I was free. Despite some of my misgivings about him, which included his gossip and his disdain for others, I still enjoyed our conversations. I had had so many meals alone that I was eager to instead dine with someone.

When I arrived, I didn't see Rico and hesitated before entering the casotto. Unlike the cozy, wooden, octagonal houses at most traghetto stops, the San Tomá casotto was a large whitewashed room that reminded me of the locker room in high school, dingy and swampy. The men were loud and raucous and didn't smell very good. Instead of venturing in, I asked one of the two men in the traghetto boat if Rico was still around, and he called Rico forth for me.

Rico apologized that he'd be ready in a few minutes. Most of the gondoliers inside were tipsy and were having trouble counting out the day's earnings, he explained. When he finally appeared, ready to leave, Rico was red-eyed and slow of speech. I thought back to the day we hid in the construction site during the rainstorm.

We walked to Rico's neighborhood in the San Polo district where he deposited me at a canal-side caffé. At the end of the day's work, he wanted to pop home for a shower and change of clothes before he'd sit with me. I ordered us a carafe of white wine and began sipping on a glass of it while I waited. Half a dozen tables were ranged along a wide street, right where a small canal turned a corner. The quaint black iron railing and flower boxes exuding geraniums gave this secluded spot immense charm. It looked like the ideal place for a lover's tryst. Certainly, that's not what this dinner was about for me, and Rico had never "tried" with me before.

When Rico returned, looking fresher and with damp hair, he asked me how my book project was progressing. He had regained his zip and cheerfulness. I mentioned that I had made new friends in the process of interviewing the gondoliers and that people had been very helpful and shared my enthusiasm. "You know I expect royalties when your book comes out," he said quite seriously. "Or if not royalties or a share in the profits, I at least expect a special acknowledgement." This was quite the opposite attitude from what I had received from other gondoliers. In fact, when I had offered to show Stefano what I had written about him, he had declined, shrugging with, "I already know what my life is like."

So I spent some time explaining to Rico that publishing a book was a difficult business that didn't always result in big profits for the author. Meeting with success was even more difficult when one wanted to publish photos as well, especially for an unpublished photographer.

"Did you take photos of me?" he asked, raising his eyebrows and his voice in alarm. "Because if you did, I haven't given you permission to use them. If my picture comes out in your book without my permission, you know there'll be a lawsuit," he finished, his words coming out in a rush.

"Well, I guess I'll have to make up some sort of release form for you to sign," I replied. No one else had cared a bit that I took his picture. Many of them even posed or hammed it up for the camera. Gondoliers posed for pictures numerous times daily; their likenesses were one of Venice's commodities.

"You know, my uncle is on the cover of a travel book," Rico told me, and I wondered if this uncle had been a shrewd gondolier who apprised Rico of his rights.

With this disclosure, Rico began a rant on his opinion of tourism (which paid his salary, I felt like reminding him). Yes, the daily influx of summer tourists, often reaching 100,000 people a day, felt like a teeming cauldron. I had heard a Venetian mumble one day about the "peste turistica," the "'peste" being the Venetian term for the Black Plague. Rico said that the tourist industry didn't help the average Venetian, so he proposed the sale of tickets to enter the city. Each citizen would receive proceeds directly from the sale of these tickets, and any surplus would be used to preserve the city.

I could see that despite Rico being half-British, he succumbed to a decidedly Venetian characteristic: the profiteer. Throughout their history, Venetians had always known how to earn a tidy, or even an exorbitant, profit from any trade. It was Doge Enrico Dandolo who agreed to provide the fourth Crusaders with ships, supplies, and men, but only for the right price. When the Crusaders were unable to pay, the Doge instead asked that they help to sack various cities and allow Venice to keep the plunder. The Crusaders did as asked, with great success for the Venetian Republic, though they never did make it to the Holy Land.

Rico seemed to have thought out his plan quite well; he had the ticket prices and profit margin worked out already. Venice is certainly more of a museum piece and a tourist attraction than it is a thriving community, with many locals leaving to find work and a cheaper cost of living. But it wouldn't survive without its tourist plague. Still, my stomach turned sour at the thought of charging admission to this unique island, like one more florid, greedy, pre-packaged EuroDisney. At least the city was still a city. Living in my northern Venice neighborhood, I had become part of the microcommunity with its shopkeepers, haunts, and local personalities. It was easy to get away from the tourists if one wanted to. In fact, though he lived a 20-minute walk from Piazza San Marco, Stefano hadn't been there in years. One could learn to survive alongside a peste.

Looking nervously at his watch, Rico said he needed to meet a friend who had certain comestibles for sale. I had noticed that Rico's red eyes were losing their sheen. He hurried away down a nondescript alley. While I paid for our wine, I realized that he was the first gondolier—in fact, the first Italian man—who had allowed me to pay for anything. Then I remembered that there had been talk of dinner. I was being dumped for a date with a drug dealer. Not that this was a real "date;" it was friends out for dinner, but even friends shouldn't renege on an appointment. Rico, I believed, was an intelligent guy and honest gondolier who treated his customers well, but honesty could come in many and varied packages.

Notice Bruno's tattooed hand and arm.

Bella Bella Bella

My head lost in a book while I sat on the stairs leading down to a canal, I had to suddenly squeeze myself against the wall or be trampled. A wooden motorboat painted a medley of bright blue, green, and red, had just pulled up to the walkway where I had been sitting, and now German tourists were being helped out of the boat and handed past me. The boat captain, a stocky forty-something man in a white hat with a black brim, was giving them directions to the Piazza San Marco, not far from where we were.

Once the Germans were safely on their way, the boat captain reached down to help me stand up, then used that as an excuse to kiss the back of my hand. He was florid and charming, his vigor infectious. "I am Bruno," he said, "known throughout the world as well as Venice." We quickly discovered that we had little language in common, but that didn't deter Bruno. It was amazing how much he was able to tell me about himself anyway, using Italian and copious hand gestures. "I will buy you spaghetti, pizza, vino, anything," he said. Refusing was not an option on this menu. He was so cheerful and told me I was beautiful so many times that I figured, at the very least, spending time with him would be another fun stop on my ego trip.

While we walked down a busy shopping street to a small trattoria, Bruno told me about his business. He pulled a map from the front waistband of his faded green shorts (where he kept several extras) and pointed with a thick, blunt finger at the route he took his passengers: from the Tronchetto car park, to Murano island to see the glass factories, a shortcut through the Arsenale boatyard to the San Marco basin, and back up the Grand Canal. I wondered if all those maps were what held up his sagging shorts under his belly. But besides just touring with the motorboat, Bruno was also a gondolier. He kept his gondola moored in a small canal but didn't use it much. At age 45, he found it easier to run a boat by motor than by oar, though in his younger days he had often competed in the regattas.

Once seated in the trattoria, Bruno ordered himself a pizza margherita and insisted that I at least have something to drink. We each ordered te alla pesca (with peach flavor), and Bruno told me he hadn't had a drink or a cigarette in years. The restaurant had a traditional setting—benches at thick wooden tables, red and white checked curtains fluttering at the lower half of the windows. The waiters wore narrow white aprons that hung to their ankles, and they yelled orders to the cook at the silver stove behind the counter.

Talking constantly as he ate his pizza, Bruno eventually spilled a bit of sauce on his white t-shirt. I wasn't entirely sure what to make of this guy, dragging me bodily to a restaurant, but he was certainly more entertaining than reading a novel for the second straight hour.

Bruno's arms were covered with a stunning variety of tattoos. Across his right knuckles he had a crude tattoo of the name "Teresa." "Is this your wife?" I asked.

He laughed, "No!" and showed me the many women's names among the other tattoos: Daniela was near a three-masted sailing ship while Sonia was across his left knuckles above a heart surrounded by a chain. He showed me his lack of a wedding ring; instead, he had a tattooed ring on his left pinkie. Then Bruno had to look at my ring finger as an excuse to kiss my hand again—he was devious, hilarious, harmless.

When I asked Bruno why he had no wife, he raised his bushy eyebrows and exclaimed, "I already had three." One was Sicilian and from a Mafia family. Another was Venetian, and the third was from Northern Italy. But he had been single again for about ten years.

I also noticed a tattoo above Bruno's right elbow, and thinking it was of another woman, I asked him what it said. As he pulled up his sleeve so I could see it clearly, I saw that it read, "Hong Kong 1968." By holding his hand a few feet above the floor, he showed me that he had been a boy when he visited China (and got the tattoo later, I assumed!) Bruno had traveled nearly the entire world, including China, Japan, Indonesia, Australia, the United States, Europe, and Russia. This coming winter he would be vacationing in Cuba and Brazil, though he planned to return in time for gondoliering during Carnevale in the spring.

With many hand and arm gestures and bits of pizza and mozzerella on his lips, Bruno elaborated on his trip to Bali. He frowned and confided that he didn't like the food there and managed to get the ingredients to cook his own spaghetti with tomato sauce. He described his nights at the discotheque where he danced with countless Amazonian Australian blondes. Apparently they drank him under the table. "Birra, birra, birra, birra," he said as his head drooped lower and lower.

By the time he had finished eating and insisted I have an espresso, Bruno was now filling me in on his family history. His parents were both in their eighties, still living in Venice. Bruno had a brother who was a gondolier and another brother who worked in a restaurant. He finished this brief history by telling me again that I was beautiful and that life, too, was beautiful.

Our waiter came by with the bill, and Bruno pointed to a young man nearby, saying, "He is the Casanova of Venice."

I pointed to Bruno's tattoos and replied, "No, Bruno is the real Casanova." Giving flirtatious compliments was as satisfying as receiving them, especially since Bruno was clearly a teddy bear. Bruno then pulled five different wads of money from various pockets, and as he counted out the correct amount for the waiter, he handed me his identification card and gondolier's license as an afterthought. His photos, only a few years old, showed a Bruno with more and darker hair looking sharp in a suit and tie. Though he was dressed more neatly, he looked too serious compared to the animated and personable man sitting across from me. He proved that life was indeed beautiful, especially if one had enough spaghetti and women!

Pulling one more crumpled napkin from his pocket, Bruno unfolded it to reveal a gold bracelet set with light blue glass. He fastened it around my wrist. When I tried to refuse this gift, he pushed my hand away and insisted I should keep it. It wasn't real gold, he pointed out, and the stones were Murano glass, not precious jewels. "Now you are my fiancée," Bruno said, and kissed my hand once again. I had never been told I was beautiful so many times in the space of 45 minutes. And the funny thing was my sense of his utter harmlessness; he fed me, complimented me, gave me a present, yet he never asked for a thing. I was pretty certain I'd never see him again.

"Bella, bella, bella," he repeated, "You are beautiful! Life is beautiful!"

A group of gondolas on the Grand Canal.

Lino lounges at a caffé near San Moise.

Lino's Livingroom

In the early evening, the colors of Venice are at their mellowest and most stunning. The sunsets may be hazy orange or bright pink or towering gray blue and filled with clouds. Canals sparkle as if they're sprinkled with diamonds or mirror the variegated buildings with watery, undulating reflections. It's the best time of day to go photo hunting. Tourists are slowing to a trickle; locals sip wine at the nearest caffé.

First, I roamed near San Marco where the tide was high and every gondolier was busy. Paolo D'Este unexpectedly gave me a friendly "Ciao, Come vá?" Franco at the Danieli station sweated in the lengthening sun and apologized that the life of a gondolier left little time for spontaneity. Our midnight gondola ride and skinny dipping adventure was the rarest of gifts for us both, I mused. I wandered off through unknown bits of the eastern and northern districts, past church after church, campo after campo, back towards San Marco. Behind San Marco is the

Rio Orseolo, which forms a large square of water always packed with gondolas. The deep yellow hotel at one end threw magnificent golden patterns onto the greenish water, like a house designed by Dr. Seuss.

Since I had visited all the major gondola stations in this part of Venice, I figured I might as well visit San Moise, too. It received a lot of business from tour groups and rich patrons staying at the nearby Gritti Palace Hotel. Gondolas lined both sides of the snaking canal to lead the eye towards the Grand Canal a few hundred yards away. A small campo on one side was littered with green plastic chairs where gondoliers lounged or chatted. I thought I'd see how the gondolas were responding to the evening light. I stood on the bridge, camera focused and poised, just waiting for the next fero to peek out from underneath my feet, when I heard "Ciao! Hello!" from the nearby bench. It came from a gondolier in a blue and white striped shirt wanting to make my acquaintance. He introduced himself as Lino, took my arm in his, and walked me off to a bar for a drink before I had time to protest.

Once there, Lino wanted me to guess his age. Trying to show his virility (and simultaneously showing off to another gondolier at the bar), Lino lifted himself above the bar in a hand press. His t-shirt strained against his biceps. He had been a gondolier for fifteen years, so I guessed conservatively at 33. "No! That is a big compliment!" he cried, kissing my cheek. "Guess again." There was no gray in his thick black hair, and his dark eyes held quite a youthful twinkle, so next I tried 38. "No! Another kiss!" I could see this could go on for a while, to Lino's glee. I told him he had to confess now, so he pulled out his gondolier's license to prove he had been born in 1955, making him 42. "Forty-two years young," he stressed, and pointing to his head and then his chest, he added, "I am young in mind and in heart."

I told Lino he had to guess my age now, knowing

that people always had a hard time getting it correct. He twirled me around while the waiters looked on, then wanted to inspect my hands. Noticing the ring on my left hand, he guessed that I was engaged, and I didn't refute it. I could see I needed something to slow him down a bit. It took him five guesses to get my age right. When I told him of my Santa Sofia friends—Max, Giannino, Stefano, Paolo—he chided me for having many Italian boyfriends as well.

Lino needed to get back to his station, so we finished our drinks and hurried off. When I mentioned that I was from California, Lino said he had just received a package from there containing t-shirts. One read, "Somebody in California Loves Me." Lino tightrope walked across two other boats to get to his to retrieve this package, which he had questions about. He also held up to show me the portela a spigolo from his boat that had his name "Lino" painted in gold. The package had come from an Eva in Calabasas, but I couldn't tell Lino exactly where that was. After showing me the t-shirts, he also showed me the vitamins Eva had sent him. I read the bottle to tell him the dosage and purpose of the pills. "Ah yes," he said, remembering, "Eva is a body builder. She wants me to start working out more." Lino was trim and lean, his bar top push-ups proving his strength, but he didn't have a body builder's pumped-up physique.

Leaving the gondola, we returned to the campo where the other gondoliers milled about or attended to customers. I had noticed that San Moise was one of the few stations that always had a ganzar, a retired gondolier who held a returning boat in place and helped the customers disembark, his hat upturned on the ground nearby for any tips.

"Have a seat," offered Lino, pulling up two green plastic chairs. "This is my living room," he added, spreading his arms to take in the campo. "Here I am 26 hours a day."

We continued talking about California a bit, and Lino said, "I could visit America—I could have a free ticket, free place to stay—but I'm afraid I'd be killed there."

"Die?" I exclaimed. "Why? And how can you pass up such a great opportunity?"

Lino showed me his gold Rolex and thick gold bracelets and then pulled from beneath his t-shirt three gold chains with huge pendants. "They would kill me for this," he said quite seriously, frowning. "How could I go there? Here in Venice, it is safe any time of day."

I agreed with him about Venice's safety, but I also reassured him that the U.S. wasn't as terrible as he thought. "I've lived there my whole life and have never been harmed," I said. "Besides, you just wouldn't wear that jewelry." Apparently by Lino's shrug, he felt he wouldn't be Lino without all his finery.

Lifting his chin in the direction of the other men, Lino pointed out how gondolier nicknames always fit their owners so well. He wove his fingers together, illustrating that after a few days a new gondolier showed enough of himself to be fitted with his appellation. "See him," Lino said, pointing to a heavyset young man with short black hair that stood up on his head, "he is Panda, you know, like the animal." Panda looked in our direction and smiled. "He doesn't like this name so much and wants to lose some weight," Lino added with a laugh. "Then we need to find him a new name."

"This one over here," Lino said, pointing to a sunburned man with intense eyes and a scowl on his face, "he is Khadafy." I laughed. "And he is Fred Astaire. See his face? This one over here," Lino continued, pointing to a tall, slim, blonde young man, "he is Lili, after Lili Marlene. And this man, he is Paololotti," he said about a short man with a simple expression on his face. "His name is Paolo, and when you say 'Paololotti,' it means silly, like a little crazy." Lino's nickname, Martín, sounded tame after all of these, but he assured me that it was a long and complicated story he would tell me another time.

Lino saw a woman in a white dress wandering back and forth confusedly. "See this woman?" he asked, nodding his head towards her. "She is crazy. She comes by here all the time. Jessica!" he called to her and pulled a chair up for her as well. I could see that Jessica's eyes darted back and forth like those of a frightened deer, and her hand trembled as she lit a cigarette. Khadafy silently strode over and pulled up a chair within hearing distance. Then Lino noticed an older man in a rumpled blue shirt with a binder, sketchpad, and newspapers tucked haphazardly under his arm. He had a bushy graying beard and head of hair. "This man," Lino explained, "he comes to Venice every year. He is an artist." There was a feeling we were all guests in Lino's parlor, watching the world go by and chatting about pleasantries.

The artist asked for a pen, which I dug out of my purse for him, and he sketched Jessica's face. "This girl, she has a special face," he muttered, quickly capturing her likeness. Handing back my pen, he opened his binder and told me his life story, flipping through the newspaper clippings from around the world and the reproductions of his paintings, ranging from caricatures of Yeltsin to a UNICEF card to a portrait of a Nobel Laureate. Originally from Bulgaria, he considered himself a citizen of the world and spoke more than eight languages. He also wrote poems and songs, accompanying his singing with guitar. "I once sang a song for the Kennedys," he confided, and he sang a few lines in French for me as proof. "Being an artist is like making love, if you'll excuse me," he said and looked over his glasses at me before continuing. "If you are always in the same position, it gets boring. It is the same with the artist. He must try always new things."

I couldn't possibly be offended by this rumpled but worldly man. I hardly noticed Lino checking his watch and apologizing for having to return to work. Glancing up, I noticed Lino bringing his boat to the dock, loading some passengers, and waving goodbye. I also looked up just long enough to see Lino point to another gondolier coming up behind him. “This is my twin brother,” he called with his hand cupped to the side of his mouth. Sure enough, there was a copy of Lino, but one with longer hair, motioning for me to join him in his gondola. I declined in favor of finishing my conversation with the artist, also secretly glad to have a good excuse to refuse more free gondola rides from Lino and his twin.

Paolo rows at the traghetto, traversing the Grand Canal.

The author got her Italian lessons with Cabrini (far right) and practiced with Ugo and Francesco (right to left).

Italian Lessons

"Sono, sei, é, siamo, siete, sono," I recited to Paolo, my new Italian language teacher. Paolo, who I had met that first day I visited Santa Sofia, had now become my friend. I had met his wife Sara and had plans to join them and Stefano's family for pizza very soon. This day he stood on the stern of the traghetto boat rowing us back and forth while he worked his shift. I perched on the edge of the boat near his feet as we crossed and recrossed the Grand Canal.

"What is 'we are'?" he quizzed.

"Noi siamo," I answered, proud that I had memorized my previous lesson. Finally, instead of them wanting to practice their English, the gondoliers were helping me to learn their language.

"I know you work only the traghetto," I said to Paolo, whose black hair was growing out again, "but did you ever want to be a gondolier?"

He squinted against the glare of the water and answered with a sigh, "Yes, maybe next year I will prepare for the test." I wondered where he would find the time to study since he already had two jobs and was remodeling his house as well. Besides the traghetto, he worked part time at the same hospital as his wife Sara to save enough money to finish his education as a radiologist.

"Well, when you finish at the university, then you'll have two jobs. If one doesn't work out, you have the other," I reasoned to try to console him.

"I want to finish the university," he repeated, staring up to the sky. "Ah, this is my dream, to be a doctor. Going to school is good for me. It is good for my . . . my soul. Is that the right word?" he questioned, and I nodded.

A couple of men boarded the boat on the Santa Sofia side and lifted on a huge motor of some sort. The boat tilted dangerously to the left, and Paolo instructed everyone to stand on the right.

As the latest batch of passengers disembarked at the Pescheria, where the fruit market was being held today, Paolo patted his stomach and said, "Monday, I start a diet. Since I got married, I gained ten kilos."

"Ahh, that always happens when people marry," I commiserated. "You get comfortable and have nice dinners at home. But dieting without exercise won't do much."

Paolo explained his plan. "I won't drink any alcohol, and I'll eat only the fruit. The anguria, it is my favorite thing," he said with a smile. This time I knew that anguria was a watermelon, not the mysterious "red cucumber."

"Will you get a vacation this year?" I asked Paolo. He was looking tired as he had for the past few days. While most of the gondoliers rotated to other stations, working the traghetto only every four days, Paolo was one of the men who was at the traghetto six days a week. Though the traghetto was government subsidized as a city service, the pay didn't compare to that of a gondolier.

Paolo sighed again and looked sad. "No, not with

the house reconstruction." Our Italian lesson had been derailed for the time being, friendship taking precedence. It was so much more relaxing to know a gondolier who only wanted friendship, nothing more.

As we pulled into the Santa Sofia dock again, I glanced over at the patio where Max and Giannino were playing madrasso. Giannino had had a little too much wine with lunch, and Max was hoping to take advantage of this and win some money off him. Their taunts kept getting louder and louder, though every time a family approached, Max still called out "Gondola?" hardly glancing up while slapping his cards on the table. Giannino kept turning up the volume on the dance music and shaking his butt between hands of the game. He had sat by me earlier, making sad puppy dog eyes, and then wanted to compare our legs. "Come look," he had called to the others, rolling up his pants leg to show his hairy calves.

Then I remembered something I had been wondering about. "Paolo," I asked, glancing up to where he stood on the traghetto boat, "is it more work to row at the front of the boat or the back, where you are?"

"The front is more work," he answered. Though it seemed like the stern oarsman had more weight to push from the rear while the prow oarsman did more of the steering, in fact, the stern gondolier's higher perch gave his oar more leverage and required less effort with greater results.

Earlier that day, I had asked Stefano why there were no women gondoliers. "Is there a rule against it?"

"No, there were a few women who tried this test last year," he said. I didn't say anything to Stefano, but I knew that having the right personal connections went a long way in how "well" a prospective gondolier might do on the test. I imagined that some prejudice existed, especially since the gondoliers were a rather cliquish group. This must have been a trying lesson for the women who strove to be gondoliers.

"Rowing the boat can be very hard," Stefano continued, defending his answer. "With six people in the boat, it is very heavy. Sometimes at the end of the day, I am very tired here." Stefano indicated his upper arms. "Also, here," he added, pointing to the water at Santa Sofia, "it is easy, but at San Marco where the waves are big, it is very hard to control the boat. Or sometimes when you get behind the vaporetto."

Knowing the American spirit, I had to add with a smile, "If this were in America, there would be some women gondoliers."

"Probably someday we will have them," he said matter of factly. He said he had no problem with the idea. "My mother was born on a boat," he said in illustration, though I took it to be a figurative rather than a literal statement. "My mother is very small," he added, holding his hand about three feet above the ground, and then stretching his arms out to the sides, he said, "and she is this big. She was born before the motorboats came, when everyone went in rowboats. She used to kill him," he pointed to his brother Giannino, still very much alive. I imagined there were quite a few sturdy Venetian women who could handle a gondola as well as any man. In fact, one of the gondola races was the mascarette for a team of two women.

Here on the traghetto, as these two men rowed, Paolo and I resumed my Italian lesson. I practiced Italian in this fashion a couple days a week—me jotting notes or reciting verb conjugations for him to check. The Italian language had enough irregular verbs that one couldn't simply apply regular verb endings to the words one found in the dictionary.

At the end of Paolo's shift, he and I sat at the table to continue the lesson. Sandro, Paolo's rowing partner, lingered nearby, a tall, lanky gondolier with chin-length blond hair. He stood out among the other gondoliers.

Sandro said something to Paolo, who translated for

me. "Sandro says that he will teach you German if you teach him English."

Besides Italian and German, Sandro spoke some Spanish, so we already had a language in common. "Where are you from?" I asked, giving voice to the first thought I'd had upon seeing his foreign looks.

"Hanover, in Germany," he replied. "It is near Holland."

"Ah!" I exclaimed. "You look more German than Italian." Sandro smiled at this. "So is your name Alexander in German?"

"No, no," he smiled and shook his head. "Just Sandro." He explained that his family had immigrated to Venice when he was seven and had lived there ever since, though he made yearly pilgrimages to Germany to visit the family members that remained there. I thanked him for the offer of German lessons but knew I'd be too confused if I attempted to learn two languages at once.

The traghetto business was deadly dull this Sunday afternoon. Often, when their next shift began, Paolo and Sandro had to cross the canal for a single customer. In the lulls, they sat on the boat's sideboards with me and dictated the verb endings while I scribbled them down crazily in the rocking boat.

When their shift ended, we pulled together some chairs at the door of the casotto. Paolo had to trot off temporarily to move Giannino's boat for him, so he left me in the hands of Sandro and an older man, the gap-toothed genius who, besides being a gondolier, moonlighted as a sculptor, painter, mosaicist, and music history teacher. He had a round, jovial face and quick smile, and he seemed to always be in a blue and white striped t-shirt. Despite his vast education and thirty plus years as a gondolier, he spoke no English, so my Spanish got quite a workout. Cabrini joined us; he was nicknamed for a famous soccer player whom he resembled, shaved head and all. Paolo had pointed out his boat to me once, a dilapidated hunk in bad need of some tender loving care, unlike Max's, which was at least 35 years old and gleamed brightly.

The three of us didn't get right to work but instead compared grammar and pronunciation between English, Spanish, Italian, and even a little German. As if that wouldn't already be a tricky task, we conducted our comparisons in my low-level Spanish. Yet it was surprising how much we could talk about. Many grammar terms are very similar, such as verb/verbo, conjugate/coniugare, past/passato, and so on.

When Cabrini saw my sorry little English/Italian dictionary, he mumbled "morti cani" and disappeared into the casotto.

"I know what that means," I admonished him, and I related to the men the story of Mimo's message to Max.

Cabrini returned with a larger dictionary that he could read without his glasses. "For him," he said, pointing to our older companion and referring to his epithet, "this is a greeting."

He laughed heartily. "But it's true," he said and explained the origins of "morti cani." Yugoslavian prisoners in Venice exchanged a greeting with their visiting family members, a greeting of entirely different words. But as is common in the Venetian dialect, the words were bastardized, melded, and translated to fit Venetian needs and humor, thus creating the phrase "morti cani," literally "dead dog." Venetians used the term for anyone or anything useless and stupid. However, in dialect the term also took on a playful air, and friends greeted each other with the phrase and a smile. Nevertheless, I learned to be careful with this phrase because it could be considered most foul.

Cabrini quickly solved my current language problems by explaining the Italian alphabet and its pronunciation and then swiftly writing out eight new verbs for me to learn. He seemed to know just what kind of instruction I needed, and I soon discovered why: Cabrini was a telegraph operator and spoke many languages, including Japanese. He may not have kept his gondola in top shape, but he knew his grammar and languages.

From this brief encounter, my impression was confirmed that gondoliers come in all types: talented, artistic, diligent, slothful, helpful, educated, and blue collar. Certainly one thing was true—the Santa Sofia gondoliers as a group were the friendliest ones around, all happy to help me or teach me in any way they could, and not just by offering free gondola rides.

Claudio

Gianni

Giovanni

I Tre Amici

For weeks as I walked in different parts of the city, I'd hear, "Ciao, bella." This was a common enough greeting, but nine times out of ten it came from a short, round gondolier in a red and white striped shirt and red-ribboned hat. If I was sitting in an empty alley by a canal, I'd hear, "Ciao, bella;" when I was crossing nearly any bridge east of San Marco, I'd hear, "Ciao, bella;" if I was perched in the archway near Franco's territory, I'd hear, "Ciao, bella;" and when I was walking around the church of Santa Maria Formosa, at the canal on each side I heard, "Ciao, bella." Luckily, I never tired of being called beautiful.

So when I was walking down a narrow street and saw this same gondolier standing on the bridge before me, I hesitated before going forward to finally meet him. Was he a casanova? Was he a gentleman? I was certain of only one thing at this point: that he would recognize me.

Sure enough, he did. He grabbed my hand to shake it while introducing himself. But before he could get any words out of his mouth, two other gondoliers zoomed up the bridge's steps to introduce themselves as well. First was Giovanni, with buzz-cut yellow hair, the build of a football player, and the eagerness of game day. Next was Gianni, with a sort of Humphrey Bogart calm that probably came with his fifty years. They passed my hand between them until it was returned to Claudio, whose name I finally learned. They then continued to pass my hand on a second round like some sort of coveted prize, while tourists had to step around us like water flowing around a logjam.

Quickly the questions came. "You are here alone? Where are you staying? Which hotel are you at? You stay there alone? How many days are you in Venice?" Claudio asked, "You have a boyfriend?" making sure he had all his facts straight, and also making sure that my boyfriend was in California. Knowing what moves came next, I almost felt like inventing a new answer—that I already had an Italian boyfriend, too—but I was never good at lying. I was also starting to tire of trotting out my boyfriend; I mean, what had he been doing for me lately anyway? Why wasn't he here? I was getting a lot more attention from these strangers than I had been getting back home, and I was reminded of that fact at times like this.

Claudio kept me beside him at the bridge's black iron railing while Gianni backed off to the opposite side. Trying to focus my attention away from the other men, Claudio offered me a seat in his gondola in the canal below us, then pointed out the glossy rats on the mossy steps near the water. (Did he think that would make me want to go anywhere near the boat moored there?) Next came a comparative analysis of the Lido's beach to California beaches, and Gianni stepped forward to add his two cents about sharks.

"You go back!" Claudio cried as he hit Gianni with his empty water bottle, making a pocking sound. Gianni raised his arms defensively and backed away. When I held my hand above my head to Giovanni's height to illustrate the ocean's depth, Gianni stepped forward once more to join in, only to be whacked with the bottle again. The hollow popping sound was probably worse than any pain it could inflict. "He is queer," Claudio said, pointing to Gianni at the opposite railing. "He won't bother you."

I couldn't help but feel a bit sorry for Gianni at this point, who with his superior years deserved more respect. Gianni approached again and asked, "How is it with your job that you can stay here 43 days?" I began explaining that I was a teacher with a long summer vacation, but I hardly finished when Claudio started waving his water bottle between Gianni and me.

As Claudio started asking more boyfriend questions, Gianni crept stealthily forward. "Come here," he gestured with a nod of the head and a crooked finger. While Claudio's hand reached for my arm, I stepped forward to hear Gianni, who whispered to me that we'd have a drink. He led me by the elbow down the bridge steps and away from the others. Claudio and Giovanni first looked surprised then laughed knowingly, as if this was a trick Gianni had used often. I felt like I had been dropped into an Italian Three Stooges act, and I wanted to see how the episode ended and which of the three would prevail.

Gianni steered me around the corner and into a caffé where we ordered. Too many beer posters and other ads obscured the walls and gave the place a tatty look. But no sooner had my peach ice tea been poured than Claudio and Giovanni appeared in the doorway, the former beaming a smile and the latter ducking his head and grinning. Gianni just shook his head and moved our drinks to a grubby corner table.

"Put Your Head on my Shoulder" played on the radio, and Claudio stood to turn up the volume. He and Gianni both offered their hands, seeing who could get me to dance with him. When Giovanni went to the bar to get a better tasting beer, he tried a quick cheek-to-cheek glide with Claudio to get us all laughing again. I asked Claudio if he could sing like Claudio Villa, the Italian crooner, and he replied, "Only for you. But not here. On my gondola?" he offered, smiling hopefully while batting his eyes at me.

"Do you know the song 'La Strada del Bosco'?" I asked the general company. It was a song I had come to love from the *Big Night* movie soundtrack.

In reply, Gianni sang the first two lines for me, achieving a decent rendition. "Vieni, c'e una Strada del Bosco, il sono di conosco." Claudio added the third, "Voi conosce lo tu," in a soft warble.

As Gianni stepped up to the bar to pay our tab, Claudio moved in close again. Pointing at Gianni, he said, "He doesn't understand English. He is from Morocco. Tunis."

"He understands me just fine," I replied.

When Gianni returned, he confirmed that he was born in Morocco but had lived in Venice so long that he couldn't even count the number of years. "Venice is my love," he answered almost dreamily, expansively spreading his arms. "It is so romantic, the lights, San Marco . . . ,"

". . . Canals, gondolas . . . ," I added.

". . . The water, the moon," Gianni finished. "You are a romantic, too," he said to me, cocking an eyebrow and nodding knowingly, reaching for my hand.

I decided to change topics by trying out the new verb—to have—I had learned in an Italian lesson from Paolo. "Io ho un amico in Danieli," I said, mentioning my friend who worked the Danieli station with them. My Italian worked! They understood me!

"Gondoliere?" they asked simultaneously. "Who is he?"

"Franco," I answered.

The three of them discussed which Franco I meant. Claudio pointed to the hat in his hands and indicated that Franco's partner had a red ribbon and always wore his hat, while Franco had a green ribbon. Gianni framed his face in his hands and said, "Franco looks very good."

A young gondolier with tousled, blondish hair stuck his head in the door of the caffé and told the men to get back to their boats. I quickly finished the tea I had been sipping, remembering Max's earlier admission that gondoliers do everything fast ("Well, not everything," Max had once added with a sly grin). Giovanni rushed out the door quickly, followed by Claudio, me, then Gianni, who each wanted me to walk arm in arm with him. Back at the bridge, Gianni whispered in my ear that I should come back at ten thirty for a gondola ride. As he stepped away to check on his boat, Claudio invited me to ride with him at ten o'clock. "Free gondola ride," he said, and I replied that I knew there was no such thing. With Giovanni now lounging against the cushions of his boat, Claudio saying, "Ten o'clock," and Gianni saying, "Ten thirty," I made no promises and sauntered off. Maybe I didn't want a free gondola ride, but I did relish the attention. I had been deprived of it for too long; Italian men were restocking my fridge, and my appetite was returning.

Giannino, Stefano's brother, pauses at Santa Sofia.

Don't Tell My Brother

Kiwi gelato has little black kiwi seeds in it.

I was noticing this and wondering if gelato had more calories than ice cream as I stood at the Santa Sofia traghetto to eat my dessert one night, long after the gondoliers had gone home. Or so I thought.

Just as I was finishing off the last bit of cone, unfortunately after all the gelato was gone, I saw Giannino silently rowing his gondola into port. The couple in his gondola were snuggled up against each other, sunk into the cushions. They obviously didn't want to disentangle themselves and leave their temporary nest.

A lone lantern lit up the wooden walkway with a pale yellow glow, but the gondola seemed to blend in with the dark water beneath it. Giannino couldn't help but stand out in his straw hat and white boatman's shirt, but also because he was big boned and well over six feet tall. His brother Stefano, of slighter build, once told me that he never wanted to row Giannino's boat because the forcola and oar were designed specifically for a tall person.

Once the couple had left, Giannino asked, "Why you no like me?" his round eyes pleading. Here we go again, I thought. Giannino constantly hit on me. I wasn't entirely sure how serious he was, if he really thought that continuous trying would finally merit success. Though it occasionally annoyed me, I generally found him funny and harmless. "You like Mimo, and Mimo is so old, vecchio, vecchio," Giannino was saying, shaking his head. A few days before, Mimo had called Giannino wondering where I was since I had never shown up for the offered motorboat tour.

"I did not go with Mimo," I explained. "Mimo has three families and many children." I still felt a bit guilty about ditching this nice man, but I knew my safety came first, and I trusted my instincts. My instincts were sending me mixed messages about Giannino right now.

Giannino kept gazing at me where I stood leaning against the wooden palina under the lamp. "You come with me in the gondola?" he offered hopefully, like the freshman boy who hasn't learned to read body language. "I just take the boat to San Felice and go home," he explained. "Is very close." San Felice was on the other side of the Ca' d'Oro, and many of the Santa Sofia gondoliers moored their boats there at night.

Still, I was filled with misgivings. The previous year I had accepted a gondola ride with Giannino in broad daylight, and he had tried to kiss me under every bridge, telling me that this was good luck. He had a wife and two sons, but that didn't seem to slow him down in the least.

"Why you no like me?" he asked again, raising his hand to his chest.

Uh oh, the sympathy tactic. "That's not it," I tried to explain. "I have a boyfriend." This was always the simplest excuse, especially with a language barrier.

Giannino tried the same well worn argument as

before. "He is far away. You are here, vacation. Is no problem. He no see."

"It is a problem," I insisted. "I love my boyfriend. He is always here in my heart." My arguments reminded me of the story Jan Morris told about the husband who said that there was only one honest woman in Venice, and he pointed to a figure carved above a bridge. That bridge, near the Frari Church, is still called The Bridge of the Honest Woman. I was identifying myself with a lady made of stone. Then again, not wanting to miss out on a possible adventure, I decided to take the risk and accept the ride. Though I didn't entirely trust Giannino, I knew I wasn't in any real danger and figured I could handle whatever arose. What harm was there, really? I was learning that kisses were a cheap commodity in Italy, signifying little, not worth much, so if he tried to kiss me, it was really pretty harmless. I was becoming Italian, I think.

A scene from *Summertime* popped into my head. In one of my favorite movie moments, a reluctant Katherine Hepburn faces a handsome Venetian shopkeeper, Rossano Brazzi, who wants to woo her. "You are like a hungry child who is given ravioli to eat," he says. "No, you say, I want beefsteak." Brazzi grasps her by the shoulders, shakes her and says, "My dear girl, you are hungry. Eat the ravioli." Venice has the same effect on me: things may not always turn out as I expect; I may not be faced with the perfect, safe moments I fantasize about. But the plate of ravioli is there, and more often than not, I choose to eat.

But right before me, Giannino instead finally backed off a bit and raised his hands, palms open, beside his shoulders. "Okay, okay. I just take you to San Felice. No more."

"No kisses?" I asked and reminded him of last year's attempts.

"No kisses," he agreed, hands now at his sides.

So I stepped aboard the boat and settled into the blue cushions. He had these really wonderful pale blue velvet pillows trimmed with rich cording and tassels. Giannino kept his gondola in excellent condition. He stepped past my shoulder to take up his position at the stern and gave a shove to the palina to propel the boat into the Grand Canal.

The Grand Canal was miraculously quiet at this time of night, about ten o'clock. The vaporetto ran only every half hour, and only an occasional motorboat went by, filled with young people headed to some Saturday night party. Few if any tourists haunted this part of the Grand Canal at night. We glided along quite silently. The black gondola on the black water was a shadow upon a shadow, negating its own existence. As we passed the Ca' d'Oro, which was lit from inside, I could see the marvelously restored ground floor with its mosaic tiles and sculptures. In my imagination I tried to conjure up a past when my private gondolier Giannino might row me home and deposit me at the steps of my palazzo. It was this kind of fantasy that had driven me to accept Giannino's offer.

"You like the Grand Canal, or you want the small canal?" Giannino asked, breaking the silence. "I take you on nice ride."

"No, grazie, San Felice," I reminded him.

After a few more meters of gliding along, Giannino let the oar slacken in the water and crouched down behind me. Here it comes, I thought. "One kiss," he said, pooching out his lips like a hungry fish. I turned my face away so that his lips missed their mark and hit my cheek instead. He shook his head sadly, making us both laugh. The last few minutes of our short trip passed in silence, and we floated into the (thankfully) well lit San Felice pali. We were five boats away from the dock.

Giannino stepped over the seat back and plopped onto the cushions beside me. He nonchalantly draped one arm along the back of the seat.

Stalling his moves and changing the mood, I pointed to the fat white columns and marble archways, remarking, "It is pretty here. Sometimes I come here at night." In fact, in the few minutes we sat there, two couples and a family strolled up to enjoy the view. Then I noticed the traghetto sign on the wall. "Was there a traghetto here?" I asked, knowing the answer already but hoping to divert him again.

Giannino sighed audibly at being thwarted and sank back in his seat. "Yes, this was the first traghetto. Now no more. Santa Sofia was second traghetto." Another couple walked up to take in the view. "This here," he said, indicating the house on the left, "was house of the gondoliers. I cover the boat now." In his voice was the sound of resignation. "You sit over here," he said, and I had to give up my soft pillows and sit on the board near the prow. Giannino first covered the brass seahorses then removed the forcola from its fitting and locked it away behind the seats. The pillows, cushions, benches, and chairs were stacked and covered by a tarpaulin. And lastly, the lantern and Giannino's straw hat were stowed in the space beneath the prow.

I saw with a twinge of alarm that the only way off his boat was to cross over four more gondolas to the wooden stairs. Giannino stepped to the boat beside us first and gave me his hand. I hiked up my long dress and carefully placed my high-heeled shoes so he could pull me aboard the next boat. Each time he hopped to the next gondola, it caused my boat to propel back against the pali, and he'd have to pull me forward by the hand. There I was, between stars and sea, anxious to not topple into the drink yet also anxious to enjoy this small adventure. We repeated this four times, crossing Max's boat in the process, and then had to step over a middle-aged couple who were parked on the stairs we needed.

But abruptly Giannino changed the mood as he

pointed to a fat, round column supporting the house on our left. "See this," he said, pointing to a carving of an eight-inch rat. "One time, a gondolier here sleeping," he said, indicating the covered archway. "The rat come and eat his ear." Giannino made nibbling motions with his fingers on his ear. "Is true," he added solemnly. I vowed never to sit there at night again.

Because his home wasn't far from mine, I strolled home with Giannino along the Strada Nova and on to Campo Santi Giovanni e Paolo, past the huge statue of Colleoni where Casanova often met nuns from San Michele for late night trysts. Colleoni, a nickname meaning "balls," referred to this captain of the mercenaries who supposedly had three testicles. This usually teeming and noisy square was now deserted and silent. "This is best campo, I think," said Giannino. "Here I born," he said, pointing to the hospital, "and as child I play here the soccer."

I tried to picture miniaturized Giannino and Stefano kicking around the ball and yelling with their friends. I imagined that Giannino had probably bullied his little brother, too, employing similar tactics to get his way. "In the day, it is very hot here," I added.

"Yes," he conceded, "but still I think is best."

As we walked beneath an unlit sotoportego, very secluded, square and dark, Giannino seized me and forced a kiss on my lips, grabbing my ass with one hand. "My god," he said, very seriously. When he let go, I had to stagger a bit to regain my balance. Maybe I should have slapped him—if we were in America I probably would have—but his actions didn't really surprise me. I couldn't help but smile (to keep from laughing), knowing he was just trying to get away with whatever he could, like a little boy stealing a chocolate from the candy store.

I looked around instinctively, to see if I had been caught. Quick guilt flashed through my veins. But I reminded myself that I was in Italy, these were Italian ways, it really meant little. And my boyfriend was back home where he couldn't see. Oh no. The well-worn arguments were starting to make sense. Venice was most certainly in my blood, changing me day by day.

Almost immediately, Giannino and I parted on a fondamenta between two bridges, surprising three sleeping cats. Giannino pointed out the direction for me to go. After a couple steps he called to me, "Don't tell my brother."

Gondola Shape

a gondola on the Grand Canal at night
so solid black
that it's like a black hole
blacker than the water beneath it
like a paper cut-out
or a light-sucking force
a gondola-shape that slides
over the light-reflecting waves
that bay leaf floating
carrying a man-image and
an oar-image
but not a substantial
real-life thing at all
just a black dream fantasy

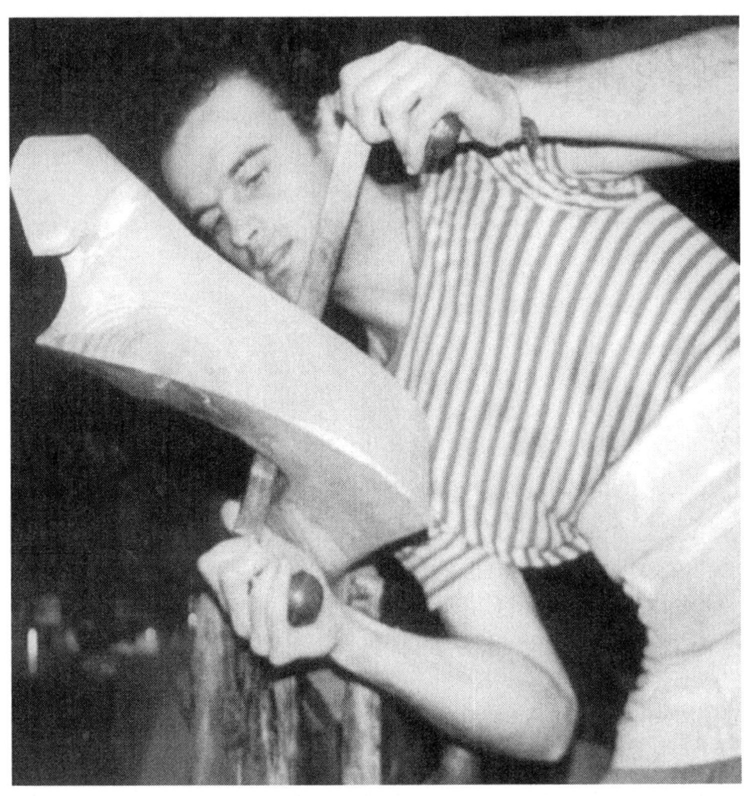

Paolo Brandolisio carves away at a forcola.

The Remer

Venice constantly surprises, amazes, and baffles the visitor.

A short street I had walked countless times, just behind Campo San Provolo, suddenly disclosed its secret to me: a remero. Though I had read about the squeri where the gondolas were constructed, never did I see mention of the remeri where the oars (a remo) and forcole were made. Granted, most of the specialized craftsmen surrounding Venetian boat making had disappeared: the manufacturers of the felze, the sartore, who made the silk trimmings and tassels for the felze, and the corderi, who made the ropes and hawsers, among others.

But it turned out that three remeri still existed out of the 200 that were registered during the late 18th century, and I had just stumbled upon one of them. A crude sign at the door pointed the way in and welcomed with "Free entrance" in six languages. A curly haired young man in a stained leather apron looked up from his sanding as I entered.

"Buona sera," he welcomed me, and to my relief he

spoke some English. (My Italian had been getting better, but I still had much to learn before I would become comfortable conversing in it.) This was Paolo Brandolisio, one remer out of a dying breed that could now be counted on one hand. His shop was very much a working one, not a showpiece factory for tourist consumption, though he welcomed the occasional visitor. Along one wall were stacked fat chunks of walnut wood, his raw materials being seasoned for making the forcole. A doorway in the back wall let directly onto an olive-colored canal where Paolo parked his cheery green and white sandolo; customers could moor their boats there for fittings. The other two walls were crowded with half-finished oars, the remi, and forcole, and I even noticed a few feri carved of wood and a hand painted sessola, the small shovel for bailing water. A portrait of a mysterious young woman hung among the woodwork. Standing in the middle of the room were large wooden vises, one holding a crudely carved forcola under construction and another a half-finished oar.

"How long have you been doing this work?" I asked Brandolisio. I was becoming so steeped in gondolas, gondoliers, and Venice that I was hungry to add to my knowledge.

In a soft voice he replied, "Thirteen years. I studied for four years with this man," he added, pointing out a black and white photo of a younger Paolo with the master craftsman Giuseppe Carli. Carli had also taught his craft to Saverio Pastor, who ran a remero near the Arsenale. The third remaining remer worked near San Toma.

"You work alone here?" I asked, though the place definitely had a sense of lonesomeness to it.

"Yes," Paolo answered. Referring to Carli, he continued, "The old man has emphysema, but he comes here sometimes to see how I do. Sometimes a friend comes in to help with the heavy work."

"Why did you want to do this work?" I queried next. I knew that it was difficult to find young people willing to apprentice as gondola makers, or in many of the traditional crafts, for that matter.

Paolo answered in a roundabout way. "Most young people want to make a lot of money, and this," he said, taking in his workshop, "does not pay a lot. Making the forcole is being lost."

"So you want to keep the craft alive," I added, and Paolo nodded. "How long does it take you to make a forcola or an oar?"

"The forcola takes three days; the oar, one day," he said. I was surprised at this because I knew how much skill and knowledge went into creating these pieces. The forcola, in fact, was highly evolved and abstract, even displayed in art museums as sculpture. Paolo confirmed that both the forcole and remi were personally fitted according to the gondolier's height and rowing stance. "It depends," Paolo illustrated, "on how the gondolier stands," and he demonstrated a boatman leaning forward or back, to the right and to the left. "Also, it is different if the boat is for racing." With this, he showed me some of the forcole on display and pointed out which boat each was used for, from the gondola, to the sandolo, to the topo, to the racing gondolino.

"How much do the forcola and oar cost?" I asked. I had read in a pamphlet that a gondola forcola was 1,100,000 lire.

Paolo confirmed this price and added, "But the gondolier pays no tax; for him it is 900,000 lire [about $6,000]. The oar costs 300,000 lire [about $1,000]." At these prices, it seemed like the remeri would have a lucrative business, but I had no idea what the overhead costs might be. Besides, if there are just over 400 gondoliers, they must not need new equipment often enough to employ numerous craftsmen. Paolo was so open and frank that I believed him when he told me that his was not a high paying job.

Going into his tiny, cluttered office, Paolo pulled some volumes off an overhead shelf to lend me. I was honored that he trusted me with his books after only a half hour meeting. One was *Forcole, Remi e Voga alla Veneta*, written by Gilberto Penzo, one of the founders of Arzana, an organization specializing in the history and preservation of Venetian boats. The other was a magazine featuring an article on Venetian boats with a photo of Paolo in his studio. Paolo also allowed me to scuffle through his wood shavings and take as many photos as I liked, and he even purposely worked on the unfinished forcola so I could capture him in action. After a couple of pictures, Paolo asked if I would like to try shaving away at the wood with the fero a do maneghi, a draw-knife, but I declined, afraid that I could ruin a piece of wood potentially worth $6,000.

Walking over to the row of gleaming finished forcole, Paolo explained more differences between them and which were for the stern or the prow on boats with two rowers. I noticed one forcola with a gap carved through its middle. “That one is just for show,” Paolo said. At the base of each forcola, Paolo had signed his name and the year, just as any artist signs his work. This showed the differences between simple manufacture and real craftsmanship. I was glad to see that this dying art was at least still gasping, and I hoped that Paolo might find others to help him keep this unique Venetian craft alive.

No More Prosecco, Pastries, or Panini

"This program is not so good," Stefano warned. "If you write Sunday, it writes domenica, but if you write domenica, it writes domenica. I think it is a stupid program," he finished, pointing his finger like a gun to his head. He had been describing the translation program he was giving me, though I now questioned its usefulness.

I had brought my laptop computer to the Santa Sofia gondolier station to while away the afternoon. Some days I pushed myself to visit other parts of town in hopes of meeting a new gondolier to interview. Other days I opted for the easy camaraderie of Santa Sofia. Since my battery was low, we plugged in the computer inside the casotto. I wondered if this was the first time this spot, in operation as a traghetto for over 600 years, had seen such modern technology. A dozen white metal lockers lined the wall behind us, and a pay phone hung on the wall, but few other things had changed in this old wooden boathouse. As Stefano and I dallied with the laptop, men came and went, talking, gesturing, tossing money from the traghetto into wooden boxes, changing clothes, swigging soft drinks. They all seemed to accept and even ignore my presence now, swearing or undressing in front of me. Stefano, who was swiftly becoming an Internet junkie, quickly took over the computer and started racing through the hard drive to see what kinds of programs I had.

Today was my last day with the usual Santa Sofia crowd when Stefano and Max manned the traghetto. At this point, I had gotten to know these men almost too well. I was no longer a dispassionate journalist recording what I saw and heard. Instead, I had become friends with them. I was too comfortable with them to question them incessantly. Besides, they must have told me just about every last thing they knew about the life and history of the gondolier. And yet they would continue to live this life, while I would soon be boarding an airplane for home. Though my relationship with these gondoliers had changed, the lifestyle of the Santa Sofia gondoliers remained the same. After six weeks' contact with them, I was changed; I was thriving on all this attention, questioning the treatment I had put up with back home, questioning what I really wanted for myself—and from a man, actually. I knew my time in Venice with the gondoliers was a game, a dream, a vacation, not my everyday reality. Yet in comparison to my life back home, I had started thinking that I had been settling for less than I deserved.

Soon other gondoliers entered the casotto, and they opened up the computer's calculator to total some figures from the blackboard on the wall. Their rising voices brought in even more gondoliers, who all added to the haggling over numbers. They were trying to divide the day's earnings between them and didn't have the right change they needed. When Stefano pulled out his money clip, I saw that he had some American dollars. He kept American money he received from tourists for some longed-for future vacation.

A few nights before, I had been to dinner with Paolo

and Stefano and their wives, Sara and Michela. I relished my new status as a friend, someone included with the wives and kids, someone invited to the local's hangout. We ate in the garden of a pizzeria named for a witch. It made me think of the children's book, *Strega Nonna*, an Italian folktale. On the menu were pizzas named for zombies, mummies, and other ghouls. But that night much of our conversation had centered on the United States.

"If I did not marry my wife," Paolo had said with a new intensity to his eyes, "I would be in America." Ironically, he had made his trip to the U.S. on his honeymoon.

"Where did you go in America?" I had asked him.

"New York, but only for four days. When I first got there," he had continued, "I was a little bit afraid, but by the fourth day, I did not want to come home."

Stefano had agreed with Paolo on his feelings for America, though he and Michela had visited only Florida. Unfortunately, neither Michela nor Sara shared their husband's intense feelings. "Why do you want to go there so badly?" I had asked.

"It is a dream," Paolo had said simply.

We had talked on about the opportunities America offered that Italy lacked—and that Stefano and Paolo wanted desperately to take advantage of. They both wanted to further their educations but found the Italian system inhospitable, daunting, and expensive. The government and universities offered little financial aid, from what I could make out, and most working class people only finished the eighth grade. Venice didn't offer many job opportunities either. Stefano had said, "I would do any job in America." I believed him; in Venice, he had worked in a grocery store, as a salesman, and in a glass factory before becoming a gondolier. Both he and Paolo had started work young, Stefano at age ten and Paolo at seven in his mother's newspaper stand. Here I was in love with Venice, and these Venetians wanted nothing else but to leave and come to my country.

Meanwhile at Santa Sofia, gondoliers were rifling through my computer's software. They acted like my brothers, comfortable enough to use my stuff without asking. They read through some of my poems and stories, betraying that they could read more English than they would speak with me. The men would laugh and point at the screen to see their names in print. Someone came in to use the boxy orange pay phone mounted on the wall and found that it wasn't working, which prompted each of the men in turn to bang on it, gesticulating and muttering Venetian epithets. Giannino, much larger and more aggressive, nearly knocked it from the wall until Stefano told him "Basta!" Someone else tried to give the phone box a swift karate kick. Next, Giannino took the wooden money box from the traghetto, lined it up along the side of the phone box, and whacked it as hard as he could. Stefano pocketed the one coin that came tumbling out. They acted like I wasn't there, or more precisely, like I was another one of the guys, just one who didn't talk as much and knew only some of the profanity.

Stefano pulled up a chair, arranging it just so along the casotto's one counter, making himself more comfortable. He already had most of the programs on my hard drive, so he instead headed straight for the games and started playing solitaire. Just like he complained always happened at home, he got sucked into this evil machine and played game after game, trying to win. I, too, stared mesmerized at the screen with him while the other men switched off shifts on the traghetto. At one point, Stefano even called over another gondolier to take a German family for a ride because he'd rather continue playing the game than shuttling tourists (and earning money?) "Do you want to play now?" he asked me, and when I declined he said, "Ah, you don't want to get stupid."

Giannino had taken everyone's lunch orders and

strode off down the Strada Nova. To my surprise, he came back carrying large McDonald's bags full of burgers, fries, and drinks. "You're all corrupted by America!" I exclaimed. "And you, Stefano, I thought you were on a diet," I teased.

"But it is good sometimes," he replied.

The previous year, Venice had been one of the world's few holdouts against the Golden Arches, but clearly it had lost the battle. When I had arrived in Venice this year, I saw four new McDonalds that had popped up in the dark alleys like brightly-colored poisonous fungi. I hoped that the days of pizza, panini, pastries, and prosecco weren't numbered.

My days, alas, actually were numbered. It was four days too soon to say real goodbyes to my friends, so I just waved "Ciao," leaving them to their Big Macs while I headed to my latest favorite sotoportego to sit beneath my own peeling plaster archway in the shade. I had come a long way since my first day at the Santa Sofia traghetto. Instead of a foreign journalist—as well as an American woman to "try" with—I was also now a sister, someone to joke with and teach profanity to. And no longer did they all "try" with me; that game had worn thin. I had gained entrée.

Andrea Pesciolino--The "little fish".

Invitations and Scoldings

A gondolier waiting for a traffic jam to clear hopped onto my stone wall, sat by my feet and lit a cigarette. Another stopped his boat to plant a kiss on my cheek and invite me for a late night ride. A couple times I was even honored enough to have one of the gondolier's hired singers wink at me or lock eyes and sing "O Solo Mio" for me alone (or so my romantic self might dream). Some of the gondoliers nodded towards the paper on my knee and asked what I was writing. "Love letters?" more than one asked hopefully, yet they'd always do a double take when I told them I was writing about gondoliers. These Italian men were living up to their reputation as incurable flirts, but I also found that my status as a woman traveling alone made me more attractive in their eyes than any physical characteristics I might possess. I had gotten used to Italian ways—the numerous kisses, the ever-present flirting, the attention, the aura of romance. Though I enjoyed them immensely, I was starting to take for granted the flirting and "trying." Even just sitting on a wall writing and here I got kisses and come ons!

On the humid, airless days, when I couldn't seem to breathe in the tight alleys, and a dark apartment room alone did not bring relief, I set off for this spot, a dead end sotoportego just one campo over from Santa Maria del Giglio. I had to walk down a narrow path into deepening shadows and under a stone portico. The sun seldom reached this narrow canal, and I would sit on a waist-high, damp, stone wall, hiding in the cool gloom. Except for a very occasional resident emerging from one of the two doors near this dark archway, there was no other foot traffic. I had originally thought this was a quieter place to escape from interaction or the kinds of encounters that frequently became delicate dances of personal defense, that, though I enjoyed them, I also needed a break from sometimes. However, numerous gondolas, often in groups, slid past my side as part of the route from either San Moise or Santa Maria del Giglio. Some of these gondoliers had gotten used to seeing me sitting on my perch and scribbling away on a notepad, or occasionally I'd see someone I knew, such as Lino. Their comments and questions and antics were often a welcome respite from writing, fun distractions and nothing I took seriously.

A little later, becoming sidetracked from the chapter I was trying to compose, I overheard an approaching group of Americans talking about the cute dog that sat on their gondolier's boat. Sure enough, the next gondola to float into view carried Chicco, rowed along by Mimo smoking on a curved brown pipe, looking more like a gentleman entertaining friends in his study than a gondolier rowing a boatload of tourists.

I had been nervous about meeting Mimo again after I stood him up on his offer of a motorboat tour. My fears were well founded. "Why didn't you come for a boat ride?" Mimo asked me in Spanish, turning down his brows with one of those looks like my father used to give me when I wouldn't finish my dinner.

How was I to answer? Because you have three families? Because you have miniature Mimos planted in four countries? "Because I have a boyfriend," I answered as Mimo glided away, shrugging and glowering a bit. I had recently learned these details about Mimo's family life from Stefano and Max, but how was I to convey that quickly in Spanish before he was gone? I felt a bit guilty, but my safety had come first. I used what had become my standard and safest excuse. I expected, perhaps naîvely, that having a boyfriend would mean to these men that I wasn't available, so they should stop trying.

I tried to push the problem from my mind, consoling myself that I was going home in four days, and I was sure that Mimo wouldn't pine for me. Then, within the hour I heard a friendly greeting. "Signorina poeta," a voice called out. I looked both ways down the long canal, free of gondolas, then up at the windows, seeing no one. Then it occurred to me to peer down the sotoportego where someone might approach by foot, and up strolled a young, strawberry blond gondolier quaffing a bright blue Gatorade. "I need the electrolytes," he explained.

It was Andrea, who had introduced himself earlier when he rowed by. His gondolier nickname was Pisciolino, the Goldfish, which matched his coloring. He invited me to return with him to Santa Maria del Giglio since his break was already ending. Though I had met many great people already, I kept myself open to meeting more, even if it might also mean dealing with the let's-hit-on-the-tourist routine. Yet at the same time I hesitated, knowing that Mimo would probably be there. I explained my trepidation to Andrea, but he acted like this wasn't a problem. Instead, on hearing that I was from California, he began extolling the virtues of the many Californian and Mexican beaches he had visited in his travels. As we reached the traghetto, we pulled together a couple white wire chairs into the shade of the thickly ivied trellis.

"Did you visit Venice Beach?" I asked, launching into casual conversation, "and did you see the gondolas there?"

"Yes," he said with a wry smile. "There was a gondolier there. But he did not know the right way to row." Andrea held in his right hand an imaginary oar. "He held the oar wrong," he added, showing me how the oar must have rubbed the poor guy's hand raw. He also told me of a Rhode Island man who was purchasing a gondola and learning to row Venetian style. "This man wants to have more gondolas in the future," added Andrea. "I think it will be a great business."

Andrea was probably right. The gondola had previously shown itself to be a successful export. During their heyday, the courts of England and France had gondolas, the other European nobles followed suit, and the gondola became fashionable throughout Europe. Besides Venice Beach and now Providence, Las Vegas had even gotten its own gondolas for a hotel with indoor canals. Maybe the world was readying itself for a future after the death of Venice, when the encroaching sea finally swallowed the Queen of the Adriatic.

I asked Andrea if speaking such good English helped him to be a gondolier. "Yes, now the young gondoliers must pass a test to show how much they know," and with this he told me about the gondolier exam. I felt that it might be rude of me to show that I already knew all about it, so I kept quiet.

Well, for a short while. "Doesn't it help to have a father or a brother who is a gondolier?" I asked.

Andrea took this question fully in stride. "Yes. I come from a long line of gondoliers. My father was a gondolier and my grandfather, and my grand-grandfather," he said, holding his hand ever higher in the air to imitate each generation. As we talked, I glanced furtively at the gondolier sitting just to my right—a woman. She wore the standard black slacks and white boatman's shirt, and her sandy brown hair was cut short over her ears. Lino had pointed her out to me earlier when we were floating down the Grand Canal, saying that she had more male hormones than female. (I met this kind of prejudice against her nearly every time I mentioned her name to other gondoliers.) She was still just a substitute and traghetto worker, not a full-fledged gondolier. I was keenly interested to find out more about her, especially since Stefano had told me that there were no female gondoliers.

The woman gondolier looked over at us at this point. "What are you writing?" she asked me in laconic but perfect English. I explained my project briefly, pointing out that no one had written a book about the gondoliers before. I added (smugly, I must admit) that I had typed up about a hundred pages in my six weeks in Venice. "That is not so much," she said. I wondered how many books she had written. "And what have you found?" she asked next.

I summarized by saying, "I have written some history of the gondoliers and the gondola, and I have talked to many gondoliers about their lives." But she impatiently cut me off.

"No, what is your point?" she pressed me. "What is your theme?"

I was a bit taken aback by her forwardness. So far, everyone had simply been encouraging and willing to talk openly about his life. No one had questioned me so pointedly about my project. Wasn't it enough to interview these guys and write a book that no one had written yet? I stammered, "I want to show that gondoliers are more than just a stereotype, that they are human, too, and come in many types, just like all people, even though people have this idea of them as casanovas." I trailed off as I noticed a smirk on her face. I decided to try a different tack, thinking that if I could get her to talk about herself, she might feel that she could set me on the right path. "I think you are the first woman gondolier, right?" I asked.

She glanced at me sidelong with disdain. "It is too soon to talk about that," she nearly spat out, and swung herself out of her chair and over to the traghetto to help ferry customers. For the first time in my many encounters with gondoliers, I had somehow offended one.

After checking with my usual informants, I later learned more about this interesting pioneer. Her name was Alexandra ("If she is a woman," said Stefano). She was still only an apprentice because she hadn't passed the rowing tests. Rico told me that she was not very good at rowing, but I suspected sexism as the real culprit. These men didn't want to allow a woman into their hallowed ranks. In fact, she later brought a legal suit against the fraglia, which dragged out inconclusively in court for a few years.

However, my conversations were all doomed to be cut short: Mimo had spotted me. He bee-lined for me, took my arm in his big, rough hand, and led me away for a drink at the corner bar. Chicco trotted along with us. I still felt a bit disconcerted about my conversation with Alexandra, but with Mimo before me, I had another issue to resolve.

"How is Campagna?" Mimo asked, referring to Max, thankfully smiling at me. I had expected his anger.

"He is on vacation," I answered, "in the mountains with his girlfriend." I had hoped to use some of my new Italian language skills, but they failed me quickly and Mimo told me I should stick with my meager Spanish.

But the pleasantries were over already. As expected, Mimo asked why I hadn't met him for that proffered boat tour. "Campagna and Stefano say you are a casanova," I said smiling, hoping to diffuse any potential anger by making my mood lighter. "And I have a boyfriend in California," I finished, realizing this excuse was starting to sound lame. They didn't care about boyfriends.

"Campagna is a casanova," Mimo said, raising his eyebrows, and together we counted his girlfriends on our fingers, "six, seven, eight . . . ," ending in easy laughter. That ended more easily than I had expected.

I struggled to explain, "I thought you were mad at me."

"No, it's not a problem," Mimo said, ordering a coffee for himself and an iced tea for me. I bent to pet Chicco while Mimo retold the "morti cani" story once again, this time to a new friend who appeared.

Just as Max had told me before, gondoliers do everything quickly. Mimo downed his espresso in a gulp and urged me to finish my iced tea. It was time to return to the traghetto, and thankfully, any conflict was resolved.

On the walk back, Mimo invited me to return at 7:30 to ride with him. The gondoliers had a large group arriving then, resplendent with musicians and singers, and I was welcomed to tag along. The anonymity of blending in with a group would provide safe conduct, I reasoned, a free gondola ride with no strings attached, but I already had previous dinner plans.

Mimo had disappeared into the shade-shrouded patio but then reappeared and pulled up a chair to join me again where I resumed my seat by Andrea. Bemused, I wondered why we needed to rush back from the caffé just to start lounging again. I noticed that Alexandra was rowing the traghetto. We all complained about the day's heat and how it deterred the tourists.

"It's good for me," Mimo exclaimed. "I don't like this work," he said, pointing to the traghetto. "It's too hot." He was silent for a few moments, then added, "I worked at the Santa Sofia traghetto for four years."

"Oh, you worked with Campagna," I stated. "And

his father, too?"

"Sí, Franco Merde," he said, laughing. I knew what "merde" meant, but didn't know how to ask if this was a nickname or another foul joke. Mimo tried to explain, but I still wasn't comprehending his intentions. With a hand gesture that said "wait," Mimo disappeared into the casotto and returned with his cell phone and address book. He called Giannino and, from what I could tell, chatted for a moment about nothing in particular before handing the phone to me. It took Giannino a few sentences to grasp that he was talking to me. Unfortunately, our conversation was rather short-lived since Giannino and I usually communicated using two or three languages, many gestures, and lots of eye contact. Besides, Giannino was with tourists on his gondola, able to give the phone only part of his attention. I handed the phone back to a mischievous Mimo. While Mimo finished his conversation, another gondolier stood behind him with a cell phone to his ear, parroting Mimo and causing me to mask my smile.

Mimo began talking then with Andrea about a broken oar. They pointed to a well worn oar leaning against the wall of the Gritti Palace Hotel. Though they spoke Venetian, I now recognized the word remo. "Were you talking about an oar?" I asked Andrea. I told him that I had recently met Paolo Brandolisio.

Andrea looked a little surprised. "Yes. This oar needs to be fixed. Where the oar fits into the forcola, the wood . . .," he paused, searching for the right word.

"It rubs against the forcola?" I offered.

"Yes, it rubs on the wood, and this part needs to have wood added to it once or twice a year," he explained. "But this is cheaper than buying a new oar." We also talked about the high price of a forcola. "This is the most important piece of the gondola," Andrea added, then as an afterthought, he asked, "Have you visited the place where they make the gondolas at San Trovaso?"

"Yes," I answered. "How many of these squeri still exist?" "Three or four," he said. "There is the famous one of Tramontin. It is behind San Trovaso."

"Is the old man, Nedis, still alive?" I asked. I had read in one of Paolo Brandolisio's magazines that Nedis was 75 and still working, but the magazine was a few years old. I wondered if I was becoming insufferable, knowing too much for an outsider or sounding like a know-it-all, a trait I knew I was prone to.

Andrea answered, "No, he doesn't work now." Mimo, who had been listening to us, added that there was still a squero on Giudecca, too. I later visited it with Stefano and Giannino when they towed Stefano's gondola out there by motorboat so it could receive a fresh coat of paint and sealant. A dull looking workplace with a gray metal shed and gravel yard, it couldn't compare to the old and quaint Squero di San Trovaso.

Customers arrived and our conversation ended. Andrea called over his shoulder that he could take me dancing if I wanted, but I declined. Venice's discos are pathetic, and though I didn't know his intentions, I also didn't like the possibility of fending off more advances. I went on my way, not thinking of my conversation with the men, but instead troubled by Alexandra's disdain and her questions.

A realization was settling over me like a blanket. See, the truth was, she had found me out. What was my point? Why was I here? My initial plan—to interview gondoliers in a journalistic style—had obviously degenerated into a farce. My encounters with them were too often about being hit on. I had given Alexandra an answer, but did I really believe in it any more? Or had the romance of gondoliers, of Venice—romance I sorely needed and missed in my life, I was now admitting to myself—superceded all else? I had surrendered to the gondoliers' interview terms; what else was

I surrendering?

Or maybe, I mused, a book had never been written about the gondoliers because it was impossible to fully divorce their story from the narrator's. The more time I spent with them, the more I was drawn into their life, into Venice. I had succumbed to this romance. It had changed my story entirely.

Mimo and Lino in quintessential gondolier garb.

Diego rows down the Rio San Poise.

Chicken Innards

"California!" I heard as I descended the bridge over the Rio di San Poise. There stood Diego, one of the gondoliers I had met while I sat in my archway at my favorite sotoportego. He was tall with thick hair the color of chocolate. I had also spoken with him briefly one day as I waited for the traghetto at the Dogana station, where I crossed to the Punta della Dogana in search of a fresh breeze. He was one of the few gondoliers I met on my own who didn't make me feel like raising my drawbridge and preparing the archers. "Are you finished writing yet?" Diego asked.

"No, every day I write more when I meet new people," I replied. I had been writing about Andrea and Alexandra, which both turned out to be troublesome subjects. As I was nearing the end of my trip, I was finding that I had learned a lot about gondolas, gondoliers, the city, and so on, so that my conversation with Andrea—though he was a friendly fellow—didn't reveal too much new material. And then my encounter with Alexandra left me questioning my whole purpose, leaving me a bit depressed because I wasn't really sure what my goal was anymore, or if it was meaningful.

"Are you writing nice things about the gondoliers?" Diego asked, grinning. "Are they nice to you? Or do they all ask you to ride with them?"

I had to laugh. Diego knew his colleagues all too well. His question also raised a tiny pang of discomfort. How will I portray these men, my subjects, with honesty, but hopefully without harming those who had trusted me? I had little time to ponder this, though, in the middle of our conversation.

On our previous meeting, Diego and I had talked about the places in America that he had visited. His English was excellent because of that. "You know, my wife is American," he said.

He told me he had captured her heart when he traveled to Chicago. "So you stole her from America and brought her here," I teased, falling into the usual game of light banter.

Diego smiled and began to nod his head but wasn't able to finish the conversation. Lino had spotted me and swooped in swiftly, like a hawk after its prey. He took me by the arm, like he had on our two previous meetings, and whisked me away for a drink. I had become used to this—Venetians always treated friends to a drink and moment of respite upon meeting, whether it was a gondolier, my landlady, or new friend I had made. Americans were often too busy for this, and at first my feminist side reared its head at never being allowed to pay. I now found myself enjoying this custom of always making time for a friendly moment, and in some of my friendships I had progressed to the point that I was allowed to pay. This time with Lino, we rounded the corner away from the busy shopping street and then crossed a small bridge to arrive at a wine bar. This small bar/restaurant had large plate glass windows that looked out merely onto a little-used street flanked by tall buildings. The white plaster walls inside and trickle of light make it feel cavern-dank, cool, and quiet. We were the only ones there this mid-afternoon.

"Why didn't you call me?" Lino scolded me. He pulled his cell phone from his pocket and pointed at it. "You have my number, yes?"

"Yes, I have it," I replied, "but you forget that I have a boyfriend," I said, knowing that this was a fruitless argument. Lino, like some others, still seemed to think I was in Venice to date gondoliers instead of write about them, and that having a boyfriend meant nothing, especially since he wasn't by my side.

"You have time for all your boyfriends," he said, "Campagna, Giannino, Mimo. . . ," he chanted at me, counting on his fingers. "But you don't have time for Lino."

"Poor Lino," I said, patting his shoulder while he frowned. "They are just friends," I confirmed. "But my boyfriend is always here, nel mio cuore," I said, patting my heart. He truly was, and yet I had felt my emerging self blossoming under attention and independence. But gondoliers didn't need to know that.

"So what have you been doing?" he asked me, wanting to know why I had no time for him.

I told him that I had passed by San Moise and hadn't seen him. I also mentioned that I had seen Mimo.

"Oh! Campagna, Stefano, Mimo. . . ," Lino crowed again. "You are a very nice girl," he added more sedately, batting his long black eyelashes and gazing at me.

I told Lino the story of delivering the messages between Mimo and Max, and he enjoyed it immensely. "Next time you see Mimo," he told me, "you tell him 'Basime i durei.'" I practiced repeating it a few times and had Lino write it down for me so I wouldn't forget. The Venetian dialect was so different from the Italian language that I wouldn't be able to look up the words in my dictionary, yet

Lino wouldn't tell me what this phrase meant. Of course, I knew it must be vulgar. "Tell him this is from Meo," he added and explained that "Meo" was a diminutive term for twin, reminding me about his twin brother.

"You know, you never told me what your nickname Martín means," I reminded him.

"Okay, okay," he said, settling himself in his wooden chair. "You know the martin?" he asked, flapping his arms like wings. "It is this big bird that flies over the ocean, always looking for the food. And when it sees the fish, it flies down and, boom, it grabs it." He continued to pantomime this bird, sticking out its neck to search the water for prey. I nodded my understanding. "The other gondoliers, they see that I am like this martin. I go to the people and say 'Hello! You want to ride in a gondola? No gondola, no Venezia!'" he called in a chipper voice. "But the other men are not like this. They have the face like the mummy." Finishing his explanation, he pulled a long face, waggling his head back and forth. He had been like a martin towards me, I realized.

Just then, Lino raised his head quickly and stared out the window. "There is Mimo now," he whispered. "Go outside and tell him 'Basime i durei,'" and he shuffled me out the door, keeping himself in the shadows.

I hurried out to Mimo where he stood on the bridge, checked my cheat sheet again and dutifully told him that Lino said, "Basime i durei." Mimo enjoyed a hearty laugh and took my arm, wanting me to go with him to have a drink, but instead I pulled him into the wine bar to where Lino sat waiting, a wide grin on his face. Today, Mimo wore a bright pink kerchief around his neck, which he used now to wipe his face and brow. He and Lino laughed like old friends while Lino explained the joke, and then Mimo ordered another round of drinks, wine for me and grappa for the men.

To Mimo I directed my question, "I heard from the Santa Sofia guys that all the gondoliers at Santa Maria del

Giglio have a tattoo," I said, pointing to my shoulder. It was nice to feel like I was becoming part of this circle, sharing their stories. When Lino heard me speaking Spanish with Mimo, he switched to Italian himself. I didn't mind practicing my other languages as long as Lino didn't mind translating for me occasionally.

"Yes, but I don't like them," Mimo said, rolling his eyes to the side. "The tattoo is a thing from prison," he explained, and crossed his wrists in front of him as if he were manacled.

I saw that Lino had a colorful tattoo peeking out from beneath his sleeve. "And you?" I asked teasingly. "Did you go to prison?" Lino became uncharacteristically silent. Mimo said that he himself had once spent a few days in jail for fighting. "Usually, I am calm and quiet," Mimo explained, "but this time I went crazy. I fought this man, made a war." He raised his shoulders in a kind of apology, then joked that the only tattoo he would get was Chicco, the name of his dog.

At this point Lino pulled back his sleeve to briefly show me his tattoo of serpents and other colorful, interwoven creatures. "I have five tattoos," he explained. Then he and Mimo commiserated about the way tattoo colors bleed and stretch as one's skin grows older. Lino seemed a bit miffed that I was spending more time talking to Mimo than to him. Mimo hadn't directly said that he didn't have a tattoo, yet he seemed to know a lot about them. I wondered what his clothing hid. They had trusted me with some information, but I got a feeling that on this topic they were holding back.

Mimo had been playing with a wide gold insignia ring whose face was nearly worn smooth. Lino asked to see it, and after inspecting it began to pull off his own gold chains and bracelets, of which there were many. Mimo explained that the insignia showed the symbol of Austria, where he had once spent nearly a year and had a woman at one time.

Then Lino handed over his fistful of weighty, glittering jewelry and said, "In America, I am already half dead because of these things."

Both men checked their watches. Lino's ten-minute break had already become twenty, so we stood to leave. I said my goodbye to Mimo and kissed him on each cheek, knowing that I probably wouldn't see him again before I returned home. I was half sorry that I had never taken that boat ride with him; at least today I felt that way because he was being so relaxed and not "trying" with me. I thought back to Alexandra's question: Was I really trying to interview these guys anymore or just be their friends?

I caught up with Lino, who had gone on ahead to the San Moise station. Diego stood there with the other gondoliers and eyed me with a bemused look. "Are you going to protect me from Lino?" I asked with a laugh.

Hardly breaking a smile, Diego answered, "You have an innocent face, but I don't think you need protection." He was right—I had remained quite safe for six weeks among these men simply by following my instincts—that, and gathering information from my sources. I still chose to believe that they had good intentions and were "gentlemen" at heart, maybe so I could feel comfortable around them. "Lino is a good guy. He is the best," Diego added, making Lino beam broadly.

"Come with me," Lino said as he led me to sit in his gondola. He introduced me formally to his twin Renato, who was wiping down the leather cushions from his gondola. The other gondoliers seemed to eye Lino enviously as I sat myself in his boat. I never tired of relaxing in a gondola. Khadafy kept hanging around the perimeter and glowering at me from under his brows. I thought this was his attempt at a greeting, so I finally said "Ciao" and smiled at him, making him relax only briefly.

Lino was busy digging around in the space beneath

the prow of his gondola. He pulled out a large lace tablecloth, a bottle of amino acids, and a packet of condoms that one of his passengers had left behind (or so he said). But not finding what he wanted, he climbed over my seat to search in the stern storage space, now pulling out a new cell phone battery and his Nicorette. "I just quit smoking two months ago," he explained, briefly chewing on the gum before tossing it overboard and making a face at its taste.

Next, Lino pulled out his telefonino again and was about to suggest that we call my house in California when he got a better idea. "Now I show you," he said, punching in an American number. "This is my friend Eva. I call her and let it ring two times, then she calls me back." He held the phone up to my ear and mimicked the sound of an American telephone ringing. When he hung up the phone to await Eva's call, he explained how he had once spent twenty million lire on a cell phone call to her, something he couldn't afford to do again. (Later I calculated this to be in the thousands of dollars and hoped it could be chalked up to Lino's penchant for exaggeration.) We also looked at our watches to realize that it was seven o'clock on a Sunday morning in California, and Eva probably wouldn't be too happy about being awakened so early. "This is her picture," Lino said enthusiastically as he pulled a creased color photocopy of Eva standing by a rock wall. She had long dark hair and was wearing a Forty-Niners jacket.

"She's very pretty," I lied.

"I told her she can come back to Venice; I will buy the ticket, get the hotel," he said, "but she says she has a boyfriend." Ah, so I wasn't the only woman who said this and had it ignored. Lino dialed Eva's number again, let it ring twice, and hung up. Apparently she wasn't returning his call this day. Lino told me that he wanted to have a son to leave his gondolier license to. "Meo, my brother," he said, referring to Renato now in the boat next to us, "he will give his license to him," he finished, pointing to a young, sandy-haired gondolier, Renato's son, standing on the fondamenta alongside the canal.

Lino and I both looked up to see a large group of Korean tourists arriving for a gondola ride. The women wore large sunglasses like Hollywood starlets, though the men looked like they had just emerged from the cave of some communist regime. Checking the numbered board, Lino saw that he was first in the lineup and invited me to sit on the stern for the ride. The passengers, two of whom were English teachers like me, held their video camera on me as we talked, as if they were conducting an interview.

This sort of free gondola ride was my favorite. I could enjoy the sights and the company of the gondolier without worrying that he would attack me under the first bridge. One time, however, Lino wanted a kiss so we could pose for a photo for the passengers of the gondola alongside us. I gave him my cheek, again, like a circus performer, doing my balancing act of staying friendly but not crossing boundaries.

Lino rowed slower and slower so our boat could stay near enough to the next one where the musician and singer serenaded the group. Lino pointed out some of the sights: the only remaining Venetian "outhouse" that hung like a box attached to the side of a building, and then the Fenice opera house, which had been devastated by fire in 1996. We eventually slid past the dark, narrow dead-end alley, deep in shadow, that was one of my favorite writing spots.

Lino's passengers complained that it was difficult to hear their singer, but within minutes we had emerged with the other three gondolas onto the Grand Canal, floating leisurely side by side so everyone could enjoy the music. Young Lili Marlene, who Lino had pointed out previously, rowed up swiftly alongside us, and Lino ordered me to use my new phrase.

"Basime i durei," I yelled to Lili in the next boat as he doubled in laughter, and I insisted that Lino now tell me what this meant.

"'Basime,'" he said, "is 'Kiss me.'" I had guessed that part correctly. "And you know the chicken?" he asked next, so I nodded. "When you cut open the chicken, inside you find these two parts," he said, illustrating a torso incision with his one free hand. "And down here, you find the testicles." Lili next to us laughed like crazy as he understood what Lino was explaining. "This is 'durei.'"

Even though I was getting used to the gondoliers' lewd jokes, I still blushed. Though it was embarrassing, I also found it amusing to be the pawn in their game of lewd Venetian phrases. It made me feel like an insider. Lili started singing in a high pitched voice, "She was a fast machine...", a song from AC/DC. Lino joined in as they sang a few verses, and the passengers laughed and clapped. This little demonstration of a singing gondolier certainly provided a different definition of "serenade!" Another group of gondolas then passed us in the opposite direction, and again Lino made me yell "Basime i durei." "If you say this with a smile," he assured me, "it is a good thing," and sure enough, the other gondolier laughed and smiled and slapped his thigh.

Lino pointed to the Palazzo Dario standing lopsided on the Grand Canal near the Salute church. Its colorful marble facade and swirling carved windows made it one of my favorites. "This palazzo is owned by Woody Allen," he told me, impressing me since I was quite a Woody Allen fan. This made sense, I thought, because Woody Allen featured Venice in his film, *Everyone Says I Love You*. But Lino added, "When he comes to Venice, he stays in this place, the Gritti Palace Hotel." Apparently, the moldering, tilting Dario wasn't yet habitable. Later I read that it's cursed, that the previous owners had all died unexpectedly shortly after purchasing it. Was Woody doomed?

Lino steered round the corner back into the San Moise gondola station and deposited the passengers, who then crouched on the fondamenta waving and filming. Lino rowed backwards and moored the boat in such a place that we had to tiptoe across wooden boards, hang onto nails in the plaster wall, and step over other boats to finally reach pavement. I was glad I had chosen to wear shorts that day, yet also I was beginning to develop sea legs for climbing over gondolas.

Quickly, Lino and I stepped into the nearest caffé for a drink after the direct sunlight of the Grand Canal. Lino had to return for the next group of tourists, this time from Bosnia, who were expected to arrive shortly. Unlike most gondola stations, San Moise most often dealt with prearranged tour groups and set schedules. The gondoliers often went out in caravans, one gondola carrying a singer and musicians—for an extra fee, of course. The expectation so many had of singing gondoliers was a myth. A wonderful novella entitled *The Silent Gondoliers* by William Goldman offered a fable to explain their refusal to sing.

"You call me tonight. I finish work at 10:30," Lino urged, grasping me by the shoulders. "We go eat, take the gondola ride, and I will be good—only one kiss," he said, and gave me one on the cheek in demonstration. "No Campagna, Mimo, Stefano," he said. I began to tell him my usual maybe when he stopped me. "No, I know you won't call me. So I say goodbye to you now," he said, and with that gave me a kiss on each cheek and a gentlemanly one on the lips.

As nice a man as Lino was, I knew I wouldn't be calling him and that he had seen right through me. But he was too nice to hold it against me. Yes, I relished his attention, like the others'. But also, if I was here to interview gondoliers, hadn't I interviewed enough? Now it was about hanging out, having a drink, taking a ride. "Goodbye," Lino said. "If you return to Venice, you come say hello to Lino."

The Best Seat in the House

I care not for
orchestra seats
or opera boxes
or box seats behind home plate.
The seat I prize
is on the back of a
gondola
at the feet of a
gondolier
in gorgeous Venezia.
Diagonal to him
I balance
to not slide off the lacquered black
and into the drink.
Stealing his beribboned hat
and pretending to ignore the
jealous glances of
tourists atop bridges,
this seat,
this most expensive seat,
cannot be bought at any price.
It cannot be bought
but only given freely.
Fifty minutes
at the heart of Venezia.
I have been honored
and desire it still.
I'll return helplessly
to this city that
grasps me enthralled,
to the seat I wouldn't
exchange for pearls.

Sandro Fandango poses happily in his straw hat.

Fandango

Crossing a tiny canal near the Rialto Bridge, who should I see but Sandro, one of my new Italian teachers from Santa Sofia. He stood out easily with his collar-length blond hair, and he usually had a cigarette dangling from his lips as he rowed, amusing the tourists. When he saw me, he pulled to the fondamenta, inviting me to come along for the rest of the ride with his passengers, so I scrunched myself in at his feet. I had had rides like this with Max and Stefano and Lino before. It was my absolute favorite place to sit because it was a seat that couldn't be bought. With just a few days left in my trip, I wanted to take advantage of every opportunity offered.

Sandro and I spoke a weird conglomeration of Spanish and Italian, sprinkled with English. Originally from Germany, he said he spoke that language as well but didn't use it with me; I understood a tidbit of German after traveling there, but the switch from two romance languages to the harsh Deutsch was too great a leap for me.

Three of his four middle-aged women passengers had bright-eyed smiles as they took in the canal-side scenery. It turned out that two of them were English teachers like me and hailed from a northern California city just a few hours from mine. The fourth woman sat mutely like a gargoyle at the front of the boat. I was getting to be a pretty good Venetian tour guide and regaled the women with details on canal tides and gondolier habits. After the linguistically challenging conversation with Sandro, it was a relief to speak American English.

When the ride ended at a stop near Santa Sofia, Sandro helped the hesitant women up from the low tide canal to the stone fondamenta, sans steps. It was a damp spot with lots of mossy algae. He practically hefted the women up by their armpits. The gargoyle still never uttered a word. Sandro and I went to the nearby bar for a quick drink, standing in the very crowded space while tourists stopped in to purchase big bottles of water ("without gas") or locals had a quick espresso or glass of wine. An eccentric Venetian I had met before was there to imbibe his usual afternoon aperitif, and when he saw me he gave me his latest English tongue twister: "Betty had a bit of bitter butter. . . ." We had a few minutes of fun comparing British and American pronunciation of the phrase. In return, I wrote out the one about the woodchuck who could chuck wood. I had learned once in an intercultural communications class that to successfully tell a joke in another culture, it was essential to explain the unknowns <u>before</u> telling the joke, <u>not</u> after the punchline had been delivered. So I duly ensured that they knew what a woodchuck was and what "chuck" meant—lots of fun for us and the friendly bartender, except for Sandro who stood there looking lost and crowded out, his straw hat slung by its elastic over one shoulder and a cigarette in his fingers. But before we left, Sandro asked for my address since I might not run into him again before flying home a few days hence, and he gave me his address in Mestre, on the mainland. I wasn't sure why he wanted to stay in touch because, besides the couple Italian lessons, we hadn't talked all that much. Maybe it was that tendency people had to say such things as a kind gesture or an expected courtesy, like high schoolers signing "keep in touch" in each other's yearbooks.

Later that evening as I returned from a stroll, there stood Sandro near the same small canal, looking for tourists. It was a corner under a covered walkway that usually got a lot of foot traffic. He said it had been slow and he was ready to quit. With a sigh he added, "But I really don't want to go home."

"Would you like to help me finish a bottle of wine I have?" I asked. I didn't feel like going home either, so I might as well pass an hour with a new friend. When Sandro enthusiastically agreed to join me, I walked the few steps to my apartment and returned with cups and the bottle and my English/Italian dictionary. We sat there in the moored gondola, sipping from our clear plastic cups of Valpolicella while bemused tourists snapped photos of us from the nearby bridge. No one ever told me that learning a language could be so much fun, and here I got to loll in a gondola yet one more time before going home.

Unlike Lino or Giannino, Sandro didn't punctuate every thought with a request for a kiss. This sort of behavior seemed to me to show his German side—more reserved, less effusive. So when we finished that first glass of wine and Sandro asked if I'd like to come along for the final night's glide to moor at the San Felice pali, I accepted without hesitation. The bottle of wine sat on the floorboards without tipping over—that's how smoothly a gondola glides, even as we swept into the Grand Canal.

This time I sat properly on the double seat, so I had to tip my head back, seeing Sandro upside-down as I asked him about a family history as gondoliers. "No, I am the only one," he replied. "My brother is a capitalist; for him it is more important to have a big car and house." He crouched down so I could hear him more easily, and I handed him his cup of wine. "My brother is going to Florida to pick up a car and bring it back here," he said with a bit of disdain. "He is doing it for business."

"That's great," I said, shrugging. "This is a good deal for your brother." Then I asked him why he chose to be a gondolier, something so different from the rest of his family.

"There is no *patron*," he replied, showing that he had an independent streak. "But the other gondoliers—I do not like them." Though he seemed to get along with the others when I saw him working, he said that he had only a couple gondolier friends, one of them being Max, which I hadn't realized. "I have known him all my life," Sandro told me, and I guessed that he meant all his life in Venice. "The gondoliers talk a lot for nothing," he explained. He made them out to be rather frivolous, crude louts. "I have only a few good friends in Venice."

We were now docking at San Felice, the same place I had come to with Giannino that other night. Sandro stepped over the seat and sat down to help finish the bottle of wine and have another cigarette. "I like this place," I said, pointing out the pretty sotoportego as I had to Giannino before. "It's so quiet at this time of night." I didn't want to get too cozy at this point and hoped he'd finish his cigarette soon. But maybe the wine made me lazy.

"Venice is a very particular city," Sandro commented. "The canals, the little streets, no cars. But it is too quiet also." He explained that he often went to the resort town of Iesolo on the coast where there were a lot of bars, dancing, and many of his friends. I had been there once and saw it as a cheesy neon strip of meat markets. Sandro lived in mainland Mestre for the same reason he liked Iesolo. It offered more nightlife than Venice. But it had its drawbacks, he explained, saying, "There are a lot of drugs there, too. I don't like that."

Sandro helped me toddle over the other gondolas to the wooden steps, and this time I felt more confident about the process. I had also decided that it was a good time to head home, before the wine made me any lazier. Sandro returned to his boat to cover it for the night. He had to bang on the wooden forcola, or oar lock, to get it out of its slot but soon came to join me. In order to keep the conversation impersonal, I pointed out the carved rat on the column and repeated Giannino's ear-biting story, one that Sandro hadn't heard before. He accompanied me home to my apartment and left after making me promise to join him for dinner the following night. I was leaving Venice so soon, and Sandro had comported himself so trustworthily so far that, though I felt a slight hesitation, I thought this "date" would be pretty harmless. Yes, Sandro might have other things in mind, but I thought I could handle them if they came up. I had had quite a bit of practice in the last few weeks. I was also thinking that this was probably my last chance to get to know one more gondolier for my writing project, so I'd better make the most of it.

My watch showed 8:12 as I rushed into Campo Santa Sofia, late for my date with Sandro since I had been held up in a protracted conversation with my garrulous landlady, who I affectionately referred to as La Nonna, though she was far more nosey and meddlesome than my grandmothers ever were. She spoke only rapid dialect to me, and although I only understood about a quarter of what she said, we got along famously. When I had told her I was going to dinner with a gondolier, she had raised her hands in praises for some and shook her finger in admonishment for others.

Sandro was pacing up and down beneath the ivied trellis, probably thinking I had stood him up. Tonight he wore a green and blue and yellow swirled t-shirt, and with his blond hair he looked more Californian than Italian. But then he confessed that his hair was bleached. I could have sworn that he'd told me the day before that he was the only member of his family with blond hair, when the others had very dark hair, but I figured that I probably just misunderstood because of my dubious Spanish skills.

We threaded our way through little alleys to a nearby restaurant I had been wanting to try. I had seen its web page on the internet in California and was curious to experience its typical Venetian fare, which meant lots of fish. Sandro was good friends with the proprietor. He said, holding his hand a few feet above the ground, "I have known him since I was this big." Then he said "Ciao" to a couple at another table who had been his passengers earlier that day. The interior was quite dark—mahogany walls and heavy wooden tables and just a few hanging lanterns. White eyelet curtains covered the lower half of the windows.

We received special treatment—a sardine appetizer, tidbits of risotto (usually only served as a full course for two), and extra service. I wasn't much of a fish eater, and Sandro smiled indulgently and laughed a bit at me as I tried to filet my sole, ignoring its face staring up at me. He finally took my plate and extracted the fish bones for me. In the privacy of our quiet corner of the restaurant, Sandro told me more about his past. This was feeling more like a first date, but I was trying to ignore that feeling and just enjoy dinner. (Okay, maybe denial played a supporting role in this movie.)

"When I was in Mexico, I was in jail for five days," Sandro said, crossing his hands in front of him with the same gesture Mimo had used. He showed me the blue butterfly tattoo on his shoulder that he got as part of the experience. "This is the symbol of liberty," he explained. "There is a tradition at the Santa Maria del Giglio traghetto to have a tattoo; everyone that works there has one," he said, adding that he had been stationed there before coming to Santa Sofia. This story confirmed what I had heard from other gondoliers.

Choosing to ignore the implications of his prison time, I instead told him, "I know Mimo who works there," and I once more repeated the story of the profane messages I had delivered.

Sandro smiled incredulously and shook his head. "I have known Mimo all my life," he said. At that moment the import of this statement didn't really register.

Next I told him that I felt bad about never accepting Mimo's boat ride, and I figured that this was the perfect opportunity to get a third opinion. "Stefano told me that Mimo is a casanova and has children all over the world, but Max told me that he is a good person. What is the truth?"

Sandro had to chuckle again. "No, this is true about Mimo," he replied. "He has, I think, two children in France, and one or two in Austria, and four or five in Italy." He raised his eyes to the ceiling and counted on his fingers. "I think that is right. Maybe he has one in Germany. But Mimo is a good man."

To my surprise, Sandro also disclosed that he had a small son. He didn't get along with the boy's mother any longer, and now the two of them lived in Spain. "This is a problem for me," he said, "because I would like to see my boy more."

Turning even more serious, Sandro related the story of his brother's death. This teenage brother was shot as he stood on the Rialto Bridge one night. "This boy walked up to him, and they yelled at each other, then the other boy shot him," Sandro said, making a gun with his hand. "The other boy was from Napoli, where there is the Mafia. But there was no motive." I expressed my sympathy for him and said that this seemed like a strange incident for peaceful Venice. "It is the only time this has happened," he confirmed.

Our waiter brought our after-dinner digestive, a

liqueur consisting of gelato, lemon, and vodka, called a sgroppino. Sandro smiled at me again when I said I'd never had such a thing before. The proprietor himself brought us some slices of warm macaroons as a treat. I loved being treated as a Venetian and getting to try things I'd never even know to ask for if I weren't with a local.

Dinner finished, we rambled around the city, all the way to San Marco and back. At this time of night, without the competing tourist crush, this took us maybe forty-five minutes, past many brightly lit shops full of lace, glass, jewelry, and scarves. I often took long walks like this by myself in the evenings. Turning corners constantly, up and down bridges, we talked and gestured the whole way. "This is the first time I have come to the Piazza this summer," Sandro admitted. We lounged back at Santa Sofia, where a woman sat on the green bench beneath a lone lamp as her man serenaded her with mournful violin strains, creating a mesmerizing, indelible image. We slouched on the opposite bench and chatted until late in the night. The other couple stayed also, and occasionally the woman serenaded her man, the violin bow flashing as it caught the light. Though Sandro wasn't as pushy as some gondoliers, I had to remind him a few times of the boyfriend I carried around in my heart. Sandro whispered in my hair, "Io penso ti sono innamorato."

In love?! Where did that come from? My first blind thought was to believe his words, but then I realized they were a means to an end. As I thought about our evening together, I realized that it was more like a date than I had intended. I was starting to act like a single woman! When Sandro whispered about his love, I worried that I had given him the wrong impression. Even after all my talk about my boyfriend back home, I realized that to Sandro I must have seemed to be making myself available. I felt dirty. Had I really been that naïve, or did I just desire attention too much? I went back to my apartment, determined to stop finding myself in the position of fending off gondolier advances any more.

Sunday morning, feeling groggy from my lost hours of sleep, I went in search of calm and peace, choosing to attend mass at San Giorgio Maggiore, the island church facing the Piazzetta. The soft Gregorian chants of the priests and the lingering scent of incense rested me and helped me feel clean again, like a Catholic feels after confession. On the walk back, I saw Max and Giannino working at a canal before the church of Santa Maria Formosa. It was a hot square next to a cheerily noisy caffé full of young people. The gondolas sat crookedly in the canal to our side. Max had to work two more days before continuing his mountain vacation with his girlfriend. "I didn't know you were such good friends with Sandro," I told him. "We had dinner last night and didn't get home until late."

"Sandro? Which Sandro?" Max queried, and I told him his last name and confirmed that he had blond hair and smoked too many cigarettes.

"Nooooo!" Max cried and called Giannino over to hear this story. "I see him this morning and he not tell me this. You sure it is the same Sandro?"

"Yes, Sandro who speaks German and was born in Hanover," I confirmed as Max's mouth dropped open. "He said he would teach me German."

Max roared with laughter and repeated all this in dialect for Giannino. Giannino pulled an imaginary long nose with his fingers. "He is Pinocchio," he said seriously.

"Nooooo!" Max said again. "He's not German. I think I speak more German than him. He's a liar," he said, enjoying it all immensely. It also came out that Sandro lived in Mestre with his wife and son, the ones supposed to be in Spain, and the one that was supposed to be only an ex-girlfriend. "Why he lie about these things? It's for nothing,"

Max added.

"Not for nothing!" I said, looking askance at Max.

"What?! He try with you?" Max exclaimed, and when I nodded assent, Max cracked up and told Giannino. "He's a casanova."

This same story was repeated and confirmed when I saw Stefano after work that day and again when I was crossing at Santa Sofia and saw some of the other gondoliers I had gotten to know. They all wanted to hear the details, and I became good at telling the story in Italian, throwing in a few "morti cani" exclamations and appropriate gestures. Cabrini grabbed his dictionary to look up the word "revenge" for me—vendetta. I was offended at being lied to but certainly not to <u>that</u> extent! Retelling the story proved to be great fun, though. The gondoliers continued to joke about titles for my chapter about Sandro: "True Lies" was their first pick. I had merely wanted to be friends with Sandro, and I naively didn't understand the reason for these lies. But over and again, the truth was confirmed. His lies, I guessed, were his way of "trying" with me, maybe to elicit my sympathy or gain my confidence. Trying always to be forthright and honest myself, I had little interest in befriending a liar. Stefano summed it up by telling me Sandro's nickname "Fandango." What a fine, fancy dancer he seemed to be.

At this point I wasn't anxious to see Sandro again, but a couple days later, on my last day in Venice in fact, I ended up running into him as he worked at a tiny campo along the shopping route near the train station. The day was muggy and overcast, oddly matching my mood upon seeing him. He eyed me nervously, waiting for the ax to fall. I was pretty sure the others must have razzed him by now.

"So, you don't speak German," I started off slowly. "Where were you born?"

Sandro looked everywhere but at me. "I told you I am not friends with these gondoliers," he said. "They talk a lot and all for nothing." When I asked him about Max, whom Sandro had told me was his childhood playmate, he said, "He's not my friend."

"You live with your wife and son in Mestre," I said somewhat boldly. At that Sandro whipped out his gondolier's license to show me the printed status "celibe," meaning single. I caught a quick glimpse of Sandro's photo, an older one where his hair was short and dark. Then Sandro looked sheepish. "Give me paper," he said, and he wrote out his address in Dorsoduro, a Venetian district. "This is my real address."

I was thoroughly confused. Everyone had confirmed that Sandro had a wife and lived in Mestre, that he was Venetian and not German. Now he gave me an address not in Mestre but in Venice itself. "I don't believe anything," I said.

When Sandro tried earnestly to make me promise to see him later, I told him it was impossible, luckily a truth since I was meeting two separate friends who would take up most of my day. Though at times the entire incident had had its sweet or its hilarious moments, I no longer wanted to be embroiled in this fandango.

Saying Goodbye

Just as I had gotten good at saying "Hello" in Italian, it was time to say goodbye. At least "Ciao" sufficed for both. But I had grown into my neighborhood community so that I could hardly walk to the vaporetto waterbus in one direction or get my morning coffee in the other without greeting the two old men at the candy store, the women at the hotel next door, the barista at the trattoria, the kid in the gelato shop or waiters in the caffés, or the gray-haired man who sold me fruit and the smiley guy who sold me phone cards every few days. Any time I ventured onto the Strada Nova, I was sure to run into at least one Santa Sofia gondolier—getting a drink, talking with a friend or wife, heading home or to a restaurant for lunch, or plying his trade. I had made acquaintances and friends. I had truly ceased to be an outsider.

Besides saying goodbye to my neighborhood, I also wanted to take my leave of the gondoliers who had befriended me. I had said my goodbyes to Mimo, Lino, and others on that side of town, but some were still spread around the city for me to track down.

I started my quest at Santa Sofia where I hoped to find Mario, the gondolier who had rescued me with cappuccino. He had promised to wear his fero ring so I could take a picture of it. I found him talking with another older gondolier in the shade beneath the ivied trellis. He slipped off the ring and threaded his green handkerchief through it as a background for a photo. But as I zoomed in for a close up, I noticed that his fero actually didn't have six prongs, nor even five prongs—it had only four. That shot down his theory that one prong could account for Dorsoduro and Giudecca. "There are only four prongs," I said to him, pointing to the ring as I returned it.

"Yes, the one is for Dorsoduro. . . ," he began, then stopped himself and drew his brows together. The other gondolier stepped forward, and there ensued a heated debate between them about the various districts. "San Marco, Castello, Cannaregio, San Polo, Dorsoduro," Mario counted on one hand.

"You forgot Santa Croce," said the other.

"That one is so small, it doesn't count," said Mario. I finally left the two of them to hash it out, chalking it up to another experience with Venetian vagaries and mysteries.

Next, I walked across town towards San Marco and found Claudio in his ubiquitous red and white striped shirt, standing atop a wide, busy bridge. He was wearing small, wire-rimmed glasses that flattered him. "You leave soon," he said, his voice more that of a friend now than of a hopeful casanova. Claudio had ceased to ply me with offers of free gondola rides the last two times I had run into him for brief conversations. I felt much more comfortable with him now.

"Yes, I leave on Wednesday," I answered in Italian. "But I am very sad," I added with an exaggerated frown.

Claudio smiled sadly. "When will you return to Venice?"

All I could do was shrug and look at the ground. "I have no money left," I explained, "and now I go back to work. It may be a long time."

Another gondolier beside Claudio nudged him and said something in Italian. Claudio looked to me and said, "You know the story by Laura Wilder about the girl who lived in the woods?"

"*Little House on the Prairie*?" I asked, and Claudio's face brightened. "Yes, I read those books when I was a kid."

"You think you can find these books for me?" he asked. "I used to get them here, but now I cannot find them."

"In Italian or English?" I asked. My boyfriend worked in a great bookstore, so I was always happy to use that connection to get books for friends. But when Claudio said he wanted the books in Italian, I had to admit it would be tough. "I'll try," I promised, "but I need your address."

Claudio assured me, "Just send it to the Danieli station, number four. That is my gondolier number." We parted with pecks on the cheek and a hug like one I might receive from a fond uncle.

Later that evening, I found Franco in the same spot. He was in one of his bouncy and talkative moods, neither sweating over pleasing the crush of tourists nor too busy for some human contact. "Ciao, bella!" he greeted me warmly. We actually moved away from the crowded crest of the bridge to stand at its base and talk uninterrupted, a flattering gesture since I knew he was working a busy spot. A few days before, I had told Franco about some stressful things in my life, including the conversation I was beginning with myself regarding my relationship back home and what I wanted for my future. My weeks of travel had been wonderfully liberating, but I was starting to think about being home again. Franco asked, "And how are you feeling today?" He placed a hand on the small of my back and listened for signs of stress before pronouncing me healthy. I hoped that implied that I'd be strong enough to face any changes in my life that I might choose to make. "I think you don't need my help," Franco concluded, cocking his head and smiling at me. "But I'm afraid I'll have to charge you for this advice. I think a glass of wine will do it."

Franco and I tended to cover more esoteric topics when we had time to talk, and today was no exception. Perhaps because I was thinking of my improved energy from walking so much in this city, we started talking about the way energy flows through the body. We then pondered what happens to that energy after people die. Franco told me of some good and some bad experiences he had had when treating his patients for stress-related illnesses. We moved back to the top of the bridge so he could call for customers again and continued the conversation in this desultory fashion.

When I showed Franco some concern for the amount of stress he put himself under by working so hard, he admitted, "We cannot be happy all the time. Sometimes there is a sacrifice." His sacrifice would some day net him a home, I thought.

His partner called from below as he pulled in with a boatload of guests. Franco bounded off to act as ganzar by helping them to the quay. I noticed that this gondola sported a new lantern on its prow, a tall, plastic staff with a glowing yellow lamp on top. For some reason, I thought of the sixteenth century edict that all courtesans affix a red light on their gondola prows. When he and Franco came to stand by me, I mentioned, "You have a new light."

"Yes, I think I am the first one to have this," he asserted. "It is like the lightning bug."

I added, "It looks like one of those weird fish that lives in the bottom of the ocean," as I made funny shapes with my fingers in front of my nose. "You know, those fish that have things on their head that glow in the dark." He apparently liked the analogy and had a good laugh.

Franco, meanwhile, was trying to find a customer. "Sicuro, sicuro, sicuro?" he asked one man rapidly to ascertain if he was really sure, sure, sure that he didn't want a ride. Another couple passed and Franco offered them a good deal on a slightly shorter ride. "I don't know why I am so nice today," he told them, "but this is a good deal I give you." Still, he found no takers. I liked Franco's high energy and was enjoying watching him in action, bouncing around like an excited puppy that wants to play.

Another gondolier returned to join the two men, and Franco suggested we have that drink. We all four skipped the few steps to a dark little bar and ordered glasses of cold prosecco. When they were poured, the three men raised their glasses and sang "Happy Birthday" to me, despite the fact that it was nowhere near my birthday. We toasted "Cin cin" all round and rapidly drank the bubbly wine. I happily paid for it, my "fee" for Franco's diagnostic services, but really a thanks for the friendship and respect he had shown me. Before I left them, I wished Franco luck on finding a house, and we shared a warm hug goodbye. Of all the gondoliers I had met, I realized, I had connected at the deepest level with Franco. He may not have been the person most available to while away a hot afternoon, but the time I spent with him was always valuable, the connection meaningful, and the company sincere and genuine.

Leaving those three behind, I descended the bridge towards the street that led back to Piazza San Marco where I saw Paolo D'Este standing by his gondola. He had his blue-ribboned hat tilted forward with the elastic strap under his ponytail at the back. This seemed to be a particular style among the San Marco gondoliers. "I leave for California soon," I told him, "but I would like a photo of you. Where will you be tomorrow?"

"At the Ponte de la Guerra," he answered, detailing

its location not far from where we stood. As he turned his head, I noticed that on one cheek he had let grow a thin spear of sideburn in an arc. The other side was bare.

"You have only one side," I said, tracing its line. "It's interesting."

"I am a geometria," he answered. "Tomorrow it will be different; I am always changing this."

I offered D'Este just a brief goodbye, expecting to find him the next day at his bridge. But, for whatever reason, he was not where he said he'd be. He had been a tough person to get to know, staying safely encased within his storied status and giving only tiny glimpses of the person beneath the legend.

Continuing on, I approached Campo Santa Maria Formosa, where I had seen Max and Giannino a few days before. It had become one of my favorite morning spots with its shady alcoves and pretty bridges and also a favorite late at night as the silent gondolas appeared like ghosts from the shadows and silently slid past on glass-like waters. Max and Giannino stood there talking to a young man as I approached.

"You call this number," Max told him and gave him some details for getting a job as a gondolier. I waited patiently to one side.

"Max, this is probably the last time I will see you," I finally said as the young man walked away.

"I'm sorry I not spend more time with you," Max apologized. "This time, I'm too busy." Summer was high season for gondolier work, but I knew that Max also had many women to keep happy. "Next time, you visit in winter. Then I spend more time with you," he promised, smiling. He was his usual charming self as we said goodbye, but I knew I'd never want to be one of the women he juggled. However, I had enjoyed flirting with him and knew he'd be a friend when I returned to Venice.

Giannino didn't say much to me the whole time, maybe resigned to the fact that I was never going to kiss him like he wanted. "Ciao, Giannino," I said with a peck on each cheek, but his eyes continued to look sad. I wondered what his version of the story would be for that night he stole a kiss.

Max had also asked me why I returned his book *El Gondolero y su Gondola*. I thought he had lent it to me, but he meant for me to keep it. So I walked on to Campo Santa Sofia to ask the traghetto gondoliers to retrieve the book for me from Max's locker. There was Paolo in the traghetto boat as usual, too busy working for a proper goodbye. He tossed me a bunch of the grapes he was snacking on, and I knew he must have started his diet. I never found him later that day for a better leave taking, unfortunately. I hoped that when I next visited, he might have finished his education and achieved his dream of becoming a radiology technician.

Finally, I went to find Stefano. I had promised to keep him company as he worked at lonely San Marcuola, that little-used traghetto on the Grand Canal near the vaporetto stop for the Jewish ghetto. The name San Marcuola, named for Saints Ermagora and Fortunado, whoever they were, was a perfect example of the Venetian dialect's seemingly illogical way of shortening names (another one being Santi Giovanni e Paolo, which became San Zanipolo).

As expected, there sat Stefano and another sweaty gondolier who looked bored and resentful. Stefano had attached his orange beach umbrella to a post to give them some shade, but it didn't help much against the blinding sun that bounced off the white flagstones. They had only two white metal chairs to sit on, so the other gondolier went inside the casotto for a while, and I sat to visit with Stefano. He had a permanent scowl on his face at having to work at this station, if even for only one day a month.

"So what is this story with Sandro?" Stefano asked me, and I caught him up on the tale. "That's Sandro Fandango," he said with a shrug and a wry smile. We chatted about my return home, and I offered to send him anything he might want from California. "You can help us find an apartment when we come to California," he said. "Maybe in a year, year and a half, when Sara is bigger, we will come on vacation." I was only too happy to repay some kindness to Stefano after all the help he had given me on my project.

"I will send you the photos of Sara that I took," I added.

"When you send those," he said, having a new thought, "send us used phone cards. Michela likes them," he said. The Italian phone cards I had seen were merely utilitarian, while some places now offered cards with great designs or photographs decorating them. I had used one in Austria with a woman in lingerie playing the cello. I also offered to look for a better translation program for his computer. "Maybe I can find a program for you to practice your English," I added.

Michela appeared, ready to help Stefano pass his last hour of work. While he rowed some customers across and then waited on the opposite shore for returning people, Michela and I chatted about anything I could find words for in Italian. I finally left them to the bright heat and their lunch, exchanging kisses on the cheeks and hugs all around.

Did I ever get a free gondola ride? I think I had learned that everything had its price, though sometimes it was a price I was willing to pay, a price that was worth it. For the price of a couple illicit kisses from Giannino, I had slid along the Grand Canal like a contessa on a dark silent night. For the pleasurable price of an hour and my ear, I had listened to Bruno's tales. For putting up with pressures from Mimo or Lino, I had received fun flirtations and attention from friendly men. For the price of lies, I danced a fancy fandango with Sandro, yet walked away quite intact. And in so many cases I gained such valuable treasures—Italian lessons, watermelon afternoons, quick glasses of wine, history lessons, indelible full moon memories, acceptance, and sure friendship. I had gained back myself. I had been losing her for the past few years as my relationship had begun a slow disintegration, and receiving such torrid attention had helped remind me of my worth. I had gained value. I hadn't found all my answers—either to the history and lives of gondoliers or to the personal questions plaguing me—but my free gondola rides all summer long were worth any price I had paid along the way.

And did I ever decide what my point was, as Alexandra had smirkingly queried? Here at the end of my trip, I looked back at my wonderful adventure, my ego trip, and realized that it had deviated down a different path than I had anticipated. While I expected to be a journalist interviewing for a serious book, I had instead been seduced (unsuccessfully) by my subjects and (successfully) by this most romantic of cities. Part of me was disappointed in myself; Alexandra's question had exposed my aim as a farce, yet I was coming to terms with the idea that I had gained such immense gifts in the process. If my book didn't turn out as originally planned, if my purpose was lost along the way, well, it simply called for a new plan and purpose, maybe even a new genre of writing to encompass it (what—the travel/memoir/romance book?) I had a feeling it might take a while to fully understand everything I had experienced this summer, but like the new friendships I had formed, time, reflection, and future trips would help me sort it out.

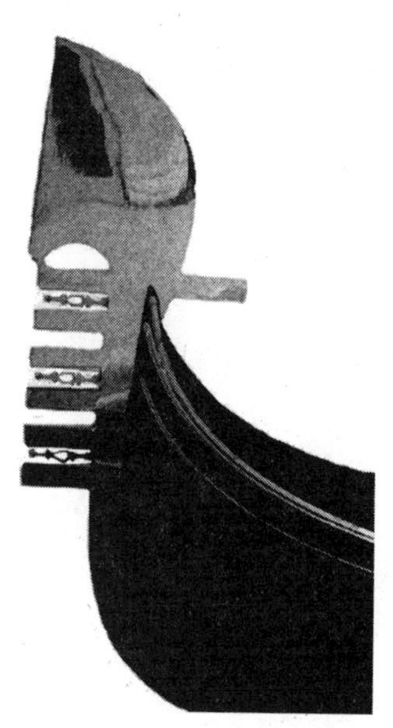

A Short History of the Gondola

> Like strange punctuation marks balanced on the golden mirror of the lagoon, gondolas prepare the complicated steps of a ballet with changing scenery which invisible, underwater stagehands slide into place. Comma, question mark, hyphen, they give the Venetian sentence its tone and its rhythm (Fraigneau).

The gondolas and their gondoliers, tied up with Venice's history since its founding, are part of its never-changing landscape. Gondolas help people pause, the gondoliers cause us to raise questions within ourselves, and they both draw out the golden day into a starry night. Legend has it that the first gondola was the crescent moon, dropped from the sky into the lagoon to shelter a pair of lovers. Repeated by every tour guide and gondolier is the custom that if lovers kiss while gliding beneath the Bridge of Sighs at noon while the bells of St. Mark's peal, the couple will enjoy everlasting felicity. That is just the sort of romantic notion so typical of Venice.

"Centuries of Tradition"

Legends like these, handed down orally, mirror the tradition of the gondola makers, who passed on the instructions for making their boats. Various styles of boats, always flat-bottomed, were used in the lagoon since the first piles were driven to create the city, though the gondola itself evolved to meet specific transportation needs, separate from fishing or naval boats. The word "gondola" first appeared in print in 1094. The word's exact origin is unknown, though it probably derives from the Greek word kondyle, meaning shell, or kondoura, meaning a sort of vessel, or even the Latin cymbula, meaning a small boat (Casa Editrice Bonechi 105).

Whatever the case, this flat-bottomed boat was used extensively in the Venetian lagoon, evolving along with its city. Although horses had been commonly used in Venice, in 1291 they were prohibited in the Piazza San Marco and along the Mercerie to the Rialto Bridge. As Venetian commerce increased and the population grew, travel by boat became a solution to busy, muddy streets. In fact, bridges that had once been flat were now rebuilt with arches to accommodate the gondola's boatman, felze, prow, and stern.

Once the nobility began favoring gondolas over horses, the gondola as a status symbol was born with each household trying to outdo the others in opulence and style. Every house kept a gondola di casada and liveried gondoliers. By the 15th century, the boats became even flatter bottomed and their stern and prow were raised, though they were not as high as present-day gondolas. The sumptuous boats of the 16th century showed the gondola at the height of its glory, with fabulous decorations from legend and mythology, gilded and silvered, nearly bankrupting their owners till passage of the Sumptuary Laws in 1562 limited their extravagance. Thus was the all-black gondola born. Later in the 19th century, Domenico Tramontin at the San Sebastion boatyard, or squero, made changes to the gondola that give us the present day vessel—changes that increased its speed, raised the prow and stern to allow quicker turning, and created its asymmetrical design, "rather like an elm leaf" (Honour 215). Finally, when economic necessity dictated that boats be oared by a single oarsman rather than two, the gondola's asymmetrical shape was redesigned to counterbalance the thrust of a single oar.

Records vary greatly, but according to chronicler Francesco Sansovino there were 10,000 gondolas gliding through Venice's canals in the 16th century. Townscape artists, or vedutisti, such as Canaletto, Bernardo Bellotto, Francesco Guardi, Gabriel Bella, and Luca Carlevarijs, depict canals clogged with gondolas. A century later, the number of gondolas dropped to 8,500, and in the next century, that number was halved. Today, only about 500 gondolas remain, many in dry dock. Similarly, the traghetto gondola for crossing the Grand Canal used to maintain fifteen busy stations, while now the city keeps only eight, some of which are used only in the morning.

Although the 19th century brought the gondola to its pinnacle of evolution, it was also in that century that the gondola began its slow demise. The Accademia and Scalzi bridges were erected across the Grand Canal, and in 1880 vaporetto waterbus service began, making the gondola nearly obsolete. The gondoliers went on strike, but to no avail. How could a smaller, slower, more expensive vessel compete with the waterbus?

Wealthy foreigners, however, came to the rescue, increasing the tourist trade and creating a new need for the gondola. In the 1980s, a German-Italian committee formed to subsidize the gondola-making trade and recruit young, new apprentices to learn the art of gondola making. Though the Venice visitor may feel as if this boat is ubiquitous, its future is in peril. While gondolas used to have a lifetime of half a century, they now may last a mere twenty years because of erosion and wear from waves created by the faster boats that share the canals. Gondolas are tarred twice a year to protect their hulls. With its strong tourist industry, Venice won't allow its gondola to disappear—not unless the city sinks first.

"Constructing a Masterpiece"

Perhaps the gondola will endlessly inspire tourists and poets alike with its unique shape and its accouterments, known as *parecio*. Andre Fraigneau strung together metaphors to describe the gondola: "Lyre-bird with outstretched neck, satin slipper abandoned after the ball, black, longtailed phantom, romantic rowboat . . ." (Fraigneau).

Regardless of the many fanciful descriptions, the gondola's shape is more functional than ostentatious. When the Veneto's rivers emptied into the lagoon, they carried with them plenty of silt and mud. Flat-bottomed, keel-less boats were necessary to skim the water's surface, and oarsmen rowed standing up so they could view the shallow bottom. A raised prow and stern meant that little of the boat's bottom, known as the quick works, stayed under water, causing the gondola's silent, splashless glide and requiring less effort on the part of the rower. A single oarsman can easily row a gondola and its six passengers through narrow canals. "How light we move, how softly," wrote Clough, "Ah, were life but as the gondola" (Honour 213).

To achieve that effortless glide remains a masterpiece of engineering. One Princeton professor dismantled a gondola to study its design and couldn't discover how to put it back together. And little wonder—the gondola is made up of 280 pieces of a variety of woods: oak, mahogany, elm, lime, walnut, fir, cherry, and a hull of larch. The squeraroli or boatmakers still follow the design drawn by Nedis Tramontin, grandson of Domenico, and kept in the archives of the Museo Storico Navale in Venice. One squero turns out only four gondolas a year, and a gondola maker is not considered out of his apprenticeship until well past middle age.

What makes its design so astonishing? The fact that the left side of the hull is longer than the right, counterbalancing the oar thrust by the gondolier who stands at its stern. This also causes the boat to incline about nine degrees to the right, for which the oarsman must compensate. The hull is 10.83 meters long and 1.42 meters wide and weighs about a ton, despite Clough's opinion that it glides so lightly. Furthermore, the gondola is deeper on the port side. When the boat is occupied by passengers and gondolier, its flat bottom creates a rising incline, effectively lifting much of the boat's bottom off the water to eliminate most water resistance. The gondolier stands astern with the oar on the boat's right side, so the gondola is usually steered along the left side of a canal; the canals are often too narrow to allow for two oarsmen anyway. (For a detailed description accompanied by CAD graphics, see Carlo Donatelli's *The Gondola: An Extraordinary Naval Architecture*.)

Another unique aspect of the gondola is its oar fork, the forcola. It is an elbow-shaped piece of wood, usually carved from a single walnut tree root, and it provides six different positions for the oar. The forcola has curves for the oar to turn the boat to the right or left or for propelling it forwards and backwards. A forcola, Donatelli points out, "can be tailor-made to the height needed by the gondolier . . . and constitutes an expensive piece of equipment"(129). With its unique design containing elements of abstract art, it has been displayed at museums around the world, including the Museum of Modern Art in New York.

Fitted into the forcola is the oar, or remo, with distinctive features all its own. The gondola oar is often hand carved from beechwood, particularly suited for its elasticity since the rowing stroke causes it to bend with each thrust. Its blade end has a slightly ribbed surface and is concave, while the wood is smooth where it fits into the forcola. The oar is very long, about 4.2 meters, usually fitted to the height of the gondolier. In general, oars are of unpainted wood, though sometimes they feature stripes or other painting. While the forcola and oar are unchanging aspects of the gondola, one of its other features has almost completely disappeared from use. The felze, or caponera in dialect, was the small room or covering created to shield the occupants from the elements and provide them with privacy. This room first consisted of a fabric covering but later was often made of wood and had a small shuttered door and little windows, closing out the rest of the world. The felze spawned many of the romantic visions surrounding gondolas; it has been described as a "small private boudoir with occupants never seen and assumed always to be lovers" (Andrieux 100). Lord Byron and Giovanni Jacopo Casanova, two famed seducers, held many a tryst in a felze. Yet the felze also elicited much darker comparisons, primarily to coffins and hearses, "A kind of black-hung tomb where you bury yourself five to six hours a day" (Andrieux 101). This was after the 1562 edict mandating that all gondolas be painted black and the felze be draped in a rough woolen rascia (or rassa, named for its origins in Bosnia) to adhere to the Sumptuary Laws. The felze existed into this century and only recently disappeared from use, primarily because tourists wish to see the city as they are rowed along.

But before the Sumptuary Laws could be passed, the felze was the focus of elaborate decorations. Gondola owners—the wealthy families and heads of state—displayed their arms or monograms on a copper shield on the left side of the felze. Gondoliers sometimes added an image of the Virgin, St. Mark, or their own patron saints. The interior was often lined with silk, satin, or leather and had mountings of ebony and ivory. The felze as well as the hull were decorated with carved putti and maritime figurines, crowns, cornices, or rosettes, and the panel covering the prow, known as the portela a spigolo, was carved and painted with scrolls or views of the lagoon. A rich carpet for the gondolier to stand on is known as the tapeo. Paintings from the past show the lengths to which gondola owners went to outdo each other in decoration and display of wealth.

"Sumptuous Wealth and Venice's Downfall"

In the 15th century, gondolas began carrying small chairs (careghin), with carved legs and velvet or leather cushions. The seat on the left was the place of honor, reserved usually for elders, women, or occupants of higher rank. They sat nearest the family crest and also in view of the gondolier in order to give him directions.

The regattas were the nobles' chance to decorate their gondolas with elaborate and fanciful designs in an effort to outshine their peers. In a letter of 1740, Lady Mary Montagu describes the lavish gondolas on display by such families as Mocenigo, Contarini, Foscarini, Querini, Labbia, Correri, and Morosini, all owners of some of Venice's finest palazzi. Life-sized statues, forests, fauna, and other elaborate settings depicted scenes from mythology and history, and were piled atop the gondolas for show. A chariot of Venus, drawn by doves, was attended by the Loves and Graces. Also gliding by was a Chariot of the Night, with carvings of four seahorses, the rising moon and her stars, and statues along each side, one for each hour, dressed as dawn and midday and laced with silver. Grandest of all was the doge's Bucintoro, gargantuan and gilded, of which a model can still be seen at the Museo Storico Navale.

Besides dripping with extravagance and obvious display of wealth, the gondola could also be infused with meaning. Legend centered on the dolfino, the "iron beak" (Buckley and Robinson 96) on the prow that later evolved into the modern-day fero. The dolphin, an animal dear to this maritime republic, provided the inspiration for the shape of the doge's hat, and it is also believed to have inspired the curve at the top of the fero. An excellent example of this correlation can be seen in an 18th century fero from the house of Dolfin, on display at the Metropolitan Museum of Art in New York. The cut-out arch represents the Rialto Bridge, and the entire curve of the fero mimics the Grand Canal. Though it differed in the past, the fero now features six prongs facing forward, which are usually understood to represent the six sestieri or districts of Venice. The prong facing in the opposite direction stands for La Giudecca, the finger-like island across the canal of the same name. Three prongs shaped like laces are often interspersed between the flat prongs; these stand for the lagoon's three major islands to the north: Murano, Burano, and Torcello. The fero leads the boat, acting as a sort of heraldic device or figurehead, but its weight also helps to counterbalance the gondolier. On the stern of the boat is placed a fero da pope of less elaborate design.

Unfortunately for art's sake but fortunately for owners' bank accounts, the Sumptuary Laws of 1562 were passed to put an end to the elaborate and bankrupting practice of one-up-manship in outfitting gondolas. Rivalries had grown out of control, and these laws seemed like the best ways to "safeguard public order" (Andrieux 101). However, many Venetians countered that the gondola now represented a state of mourning for the city's lost liberties, for it was decreed that the gondola be entirely painted and outfitted in black.

The new laws were quite detailed yet failed to include a few specific items: boat hooks, lanterns or flowers and their holder. These features remain ornate even today. The boathooks usually come in the shape of a triton, seahorse, or mermaid, and now a lantern may be replaced by a flag, eagle, or other statuette. In the past, any gondolier who did not follow the edicts and continued to steer a showy gondola faced three years in the galleys as punishment. However, the laws exempted the doges and the embassy, who continued to use boats of any color and elaborate decoration, the Bucintoro being the prime example.

"The Boats of Death"

When the magistrates passed the Sumptuary Laws, they could never have suspected the many comparisons later writers would make regarding the gondola's new color scheme. Even though Venetian coffins had been traditionally draped in red, hearse boats were painted red, and the undertaker's helpers wore red on the journey to the cemetery island of San Michele, the rest of the world has erupted in countless descriptions of hearses and death. In *Death in Venice*, Thomas Mann writes of the gondola as being "Black as nothing else on earth except a coffin . . . what visions of death itself, the bier and solemn rites and last soundless voyage" (Mann 21). This tumbles forth in the same breath as when Mann's character Aschenbach says the gondola is the "most luxurious, most relaxing seat in the world."

The poet Percy Bysshe Shelley earlier compared the gondola to "moths of which the coffin might have been the chrysalis" (Buckley and Robinson 97). Certainly the Romantic poets had their gloomy side. Andre Fraigneau, adding just a spark of glee in this contradiction, described the gondola as a "coffin of happiness." The well traveled Wright Morris carried out this elaborate metaphor, topping them all, when he wrote,

> The gondola casts a black ominous shadow on the water. Gleaming black, [it] puts the observer in mind of a watery hearse. Black. Why must the gondola be black? It is less a color than a state of soul, it appeals and gratifies below the level of discussion. Limousines are black, hearses are black, and black is the color of authority, mystery, and death. . . its appropriate aura of eternal mourning (Morris, Wright).

Perhaps just a slight exaggeration of symbolism, that.

"Not Merely Transportation"

Obviously, the gondola's main purpose is as a means of transportation. The classic black gondola is a staple of the tourist industry, with ten official gondola stands in the city and countless small ones beside numerous canals. But at $15,000 to $20,000 on up for a fully outfitted gondola, private citizens can no longer afford to own them. Most gondolas today not used in the tourist trade are destined for the lakes of foreign millionaires, though some businesses still own them for use on festival occasions.

Furthermore, larger, wider gondolas with two oarsmen are used as traghetti to ferry people across the Grand Canal in the absence of bridges. The first traghetto was created at San Beneto in 1293, and the oldest traghetto still in operation since 1298 is at San Barnaba. The traghetti served a social function as well, where public notices were posted. The gondoliers who worked the traghetti often formed a brotherhood, known as a fraglia, with its own chief, magistrates, and patron saint. Venetians generally stand while crossing in the traghetto, though this vision has been likened to the souls of the dead crossing the River Styx (Morris, Wright). Other boats similar to the gondola, particularly the sandolo or puparino, are used to deliver produce or goods within the city or as hearses to carry the dead to San Michele.

Though the gondola is primarily a mode of transportation, it has other uses as well. Gondolas are used in races and regattas, including many of the city's major festivals such as the Regata Storica, the Feast of the Redentore, and Venice's Marriage to the Sea. Poets and singers have been inspired by the gondola for centuries, including "La Biondina in gondoleta," written for the noble Marina Querini-Benzon. Gondolas have inspired operas and symphonies and even a Gilbert and Sullivan musical. Certainly, though, the gondola is the conveyance of choice for lovers. Countless trysts and escapades have occurred in the privacy of a gondola, and Alfred de Musset once said, "People can't say they've explored all the mysteries of love unless they've been in a gondola on a moonlit night" (Honour 216).

"That Splashless Glide"

"An old dancing slipper gliding over quiet waters, propelled by a man standing up and leaning on a matchstick" (Fraigneau)—thus have the gondola and its oarsman been described as he rows his gondola. The "Venetian stroke" and rowing style are unique among rowed craft and take time to master. The gondolier stands at the back of the boat so he may view the water below (and in the past peer over the felze), and he pushes the oar with his whole weight tipped forward, necessitating great balance and an unsafe stance. Henry James believed the movement of a rowing gondolier was awkward and graceful at the same time, having "the boldness of a plunging bird and the regularity of a pendulum" (James 15). On his visit to Venice, Mark Twain wrote,

> Against [the forcola] the gondolier takes a purchase with his oar, changing it at intervals to the other side of the peg or dropping it into another of the crooks, as the steering of the craft may demand—and how in the world he can back and fill, shoot straight ahead, or flirt suddenly around a corner, and make the oar stay in those insignificant notches is a problem to me and a never-diminishing matter of interest (Twain 190).

These basic rowing techniques Twain mentions have been used for centuries.

Despite its awkward appearance and difficulties, rowing actually requires grace and confidence. Young noblemen often apprenticed themselves to gondoliers to learn the technique and increase their elegance. Pushing the oar forward causes the boat to veer to the left, while a dragging motion causes it to turn right. Besides pushing the oar against water to propel the boat, the gondolier also occasionally prods it against the canal bottom or the sides of buildings. The gondolier perfects his stroke, causing hardly a splash and creating a fluid, gliding sensation.

Regardless of the great skill, collisions can still occur. The canals are narrow and have many blind corners, so the gondoliers call out to each other in warning using the Venetian dialect. "Oeeee!" warns "Look out!" "Si a longo!" means straight ahead or advises others to use the brake to stop the gondola. "Premando!" means "We are going left," and "Stagando!" means "We are going right." Some directional signs are posted on the canals to direct traffic, but the gondoliers rely primarily on their strong voices, which some listeners have ungenerously described as a "wailing noise in incomprehensible jargon" (Andrieux 103).

"The Sophisticated Taxi Driver"

Not only have gondolas been glorified over the centuries, but so have their gondoliers. They are considered inherently romantic, the fantasy objects of tourists and last hope for middle-aged women. In the past, they were rowers and boatkeepers, but traditionally they also knew the best addresses and back staircases in order to act as go-betweens for their masters. It is maintained that they never took bribes and never betrayed their masters after illicit intrigues, fearing late night drowning by their colleagues. Henry James described the gondolier as having "a kind of nobleness which suggests an image on a Greek frieze" (James 15).

Furthermore, in the past gondoliers were also known as the best fist fighters, requiring that their masters give them Sundays off to display their prowess at the local bridges. The Ponte della Paglia just behind the Palazzo Ducale was named for its public fights. In fact, a carving of the Madonna of the Gondoliers can be seen on the bridge's base facing the basin. The bridge originally had no balustrade, and fighters battled to knock each other into the canal or back their opponents off the bridge. These fights were great public spectacles, yet they also helped keep the gondoliers fit and in competitive shape.

After public fighting was banned, the gondoliers turned to other amusements, such as regattas as a show of their strength and skill. Interestingly, they also participated in a game called the "Forces of Hercules." Often there was competition between the two sides of the city: the Castellani made up of the Castello, San Marco, and Dorsoduro districts, and the Nicolotti made up of San Polo, Cannaregio, and Santa Croce. For this event, boats were strung together and planks placed atop them to form a platform for costumed or even nearly naked gondoliers to build a human pyramid. Paintings from the 18th century show as many as 51 men using planks and prodigious strength to form a successful pyramid. Onlookers were awed as a child crowned the top holding a bird, but the "Forces of Hercules" often ended with a splash into the canal.

Of course, gondoliers didn't usually appear in public naked. In the past, most gondoliers wore a plain shirt, wide sash, and small cap, and those in private service appeared in livery. Foreign or government service gondoliers bedecked themselves with gold and silver trimmings, and for the regattas they disguised themselves as Persians, Turks, and Hussars or adorned themselves in gold-laced red velvet jackets and large hats, costumes for show only and impractical for everyday rowing. Nowadays, their traditional uniform consists of a red and white striped or blue and white striped jersey or white sailor's shirt, black slacks, and a beribboned hat. The stripes traditionally symbolized the colors of the household, as also seen on the wooden pali where gondolas were moored before palazzi.

Gondoliers were always a colorful bunch, and their voices were great assets. Crying out warnings, singing, insulting each other, abusing actors at the local theater, or simply plying their trade, their voices have been remarked on by many. James noted, "The voice of the gondolier is in fact for audibility the dominant or rather the only note of Venice" (James 16). In the past, gondoliers generally received a good musical education at the theater, which was inexpensive and open to the public. Playwright Carlo Goldoni even arranged free entrance for many of them. They sang to accompany the movement of the oars or sang out duets across the wide canals, alternating lines of Torquato Tasso's *Gerusalemme Liberata* or other operas. Goethe remarked on the experience of hearing these songs late at night, and Wagner was apparently inspired by their singing to use it in the third act of *Tristan and Isolde*. At least two gondoliers, Giovanni Sibillato and Antonio Bianchi, went on to sing for the doge or other nobles and officials. However, contemporary gondoliers do not live up to this stereotype; in order to hear singing in a gondola, tourists must hire professionals.

In contrast, the gondoliers were also known as masters of insult, haranguing each other with "Your saint's a washout!" or "Your madonna's a whore!" "Claques" were organized to attend the theater specifically to boo or cheer at the plays. Most of those traditions have passed away, though any modern visitor to Venice will be familiar with the cry "Gondola! Gondola!" as the boatmen try to lure customers. Mary McCarthy summed up this sound, stating that "It comes to seem like an obscene suggestion" (McCarthy 142).

Yet despite any complaints against them, the gondoliers have proven most often to be objects of love or admiration. Helen Radnor fell in love with her gondolier Giovanni Fasan and brought him home to England to row her down the Thames. John Addington Symonds was inseparable from Angelo Fusato, his gondolier, and Symond's indulgent wife even provided for Fusato after her husband's death. Perhaps the greatest known and most vociferous adorer of gondoliers was Frederick Rolfe, also known as Baron Corvo, whose *Desire and Pursuit of the Whole* is a thinly veiled autobiography about his Venetian exploits and love for an asexual gondolier. He gushed that gondoliers have

> The noble firm necks, the opulent shoulders, the stalwart arms, the utterly magnificent breasts, the lithely muscular bodies inserted in (and springing from) the well-compacted hips, the long, slim, sinewy-rounded legs, the large, agile, sensible feet

> of that immortal youth to which Hellas once gave diadems (Honour 216).

Corvo must have made quite a study of his subjects. The only detail he left out is the tradition that gondoliers have webbed feet, hence they never remove their shoes before strangers. Henry James admired these boatmen as well, saying, "He is a part of your daily life, your double, your shadow, your complement" (James 15). Certainly, gondoliers have developed a unique place for themselves in Venice's long history.

Glossary

I have generally used the traditional Venetian spellings of words, particularly for street and canal references. Sometimes I found two to three spellings of particular words; I agree with J.G. Links, who said, "Consistency is not a virtue held very high by Venetians" (246). In general, I have used the Italian spelling of plural nouns for any Italian words included in the text, such as gondola/gondole, traghetto/traghetti, and palino/pali.

acqua alta "high water;" refers to periodic flooding of Venice.

anguria watermelon.

barcarolle boatman's song.

bella beautiful.

birra beer.

Bucintoro ceremonial barge of the doge.

buon giorno good day.

calle a long, narrow street.

campo square; open area surrounded by buildings often a meeting place for neighbors, usually named for the nearby church.

campiello a small campo.

caorlina a long boat rowed by six standing men.

caponera felze in Venetian dialect.

cappuccino espresso served with steamed milk.

careghin small, carved chairs in the gondola; also known as the seggioline.

casanova a man known as a great lover and seducer of women, named for Giovanni Jacopo Casanova, who was born in Venice and lived from 1725 to1798.

casotto small building used by gondoliers to store their belongings when working; usually wooden and eight-sided.

cavalier servente also known as the cicisbeo, a wife's lover who was an accepted part of the household, escorting the woman and attending her, with the implied assent of the husband.

corderi makers of ropes and hawsers.

cornuto bearing cuckold's horns.

corte court or small open space surrounded by buildings, and usually having no exit.

doge the chief magistrate in the former republic of Venice.

dolfino another name for the fero, refering to its shape like a dolfin's head.

felze a cloth or wooden cabin on a gondola of the past.

fero the prow ironwork; it serves an ornamental purpose as well as balancing the weight of the gondolier; popularly spelled "ferro" in Italian.

fero a do maneghi a draw knife used to carve and shape

	the forcola.
fero da pope	the ornamental stern ironwork.
fodra	a rectangular board on the side of the gondola near the seat.
fondamenta	literally "foundation;" refers to a wide walkway alongside a major canal.
forcola	oar fork, where the gondolier rests the oar while rowing.
fraglia	a brotherhood of gondoliers.
ganzar	retired gondolier who helps passengers on and off the gondola.
gelato	Italian style ice cream (ice cream was invented in Italy).
gondola di casada	"gondola of the house" kept by Venetian nobility.
gondolino	a slim racing gondola.
grappa	a liqueur.
innamorato	in love.
insalata mista	salad of mixed greens.
lira	Italian currency before the Euro.
madrasso	Venetian card game.
mascarette	a boat rowed by two women.
melone	melon, including cantaloupe and honeydew.
Mercerie	the area of shops between Rialto and Piazza S. Marco.
Oeeee!	"Look out!" warning when a gondolier approaches a blind turn.
palino/pali	(plural) wooden posts driven into the canal bottom for mooring boats.
palazzi	palaces.
panini	sandwiches.
parecio	gondola accouterments, such as the boat hooks, lanterns, cushions, chairs, and rugs.

patron	boss.
piazza	a large square; in Venice, piazza only refers to the Piazza San Marco.
ponte	bridge.
portela a spigolo	the wooden panel covering the opening to the space under the prow; it is usually painted or carved.
prosecco	a light, bubbly white wine, like champagne.
puparino	a small rowed boat.
pusiol	a curved board on the side of the gondola to which the boathooks are attached.
putti	cherubs or angels.
regatta	boat race (spelled "regata" in Venetian dialect).
remer	oar and forcola maker.
remeri	oar making shop.
remo	oar.
risotto	seasoned rice cooked in stock.
rostro	Venetian dialect for the fero.
sandolo	boat smaller than a gondola, rowed by one standing oarsman.
sartore	makers of silk trimmings and tassels for the felze.
sessola	small shovel for bailing water out of the gondola.
sestieri	the districts of Venice (San Polo, Cannaregio, Santa Croce, Castello, San Marco, and Dorsoduro).
sgroppino	an after dinner drink containing gelato and vodka; the word literally means "vomit."
signora	title of address for a married or older woman.
sopranome	nickname.
sotoportego	a passageway or small street entered through an archway and often covered.
sottomarino	black paint for the gondola.
squeraroli	gondola makers.

squero boatyard where gondolas are made.

tapeo the carpet on the gondola's stern where the gondolier stands.

teza building where the gondola is constructed.

traghetto the gondola station where people may hire a gondola or cross the Grand Canal; the term also refers to the larger, unadorned gondola used to ferry passengers across the canal.

trattoria restaurant.

vaporetto the public transportation waterbus.

vedutisti Venetian townscape artists, such as Canaletto, Bernardo Bellotto, Francesco Guardi, and Gabriel Bella.

Veneto the mainland region near Venice.

vino wine.

Bibliography

Andrieux, Maurice. *Daily Life in Venice in the Time of Casanova.* translated by Mary Fitton. New York: Praegar Publishers, 1969.

Brion, Marcel. *Venice: The Masque of Italy.* London: Elek Books, 1962.

Brodkey, Harold. *My Venice.* New York: Metropolitan Books, 1998.

Buckley, Jonathan and Hilary Robinson. *Venice: The Rough Guide.* London: Rough Guides Ltd., 1995.

Caniato, Giovanni. "Venetian Boats: A Heritage to be Preserved." *Ligabue Magazine.* Anno XV, Number 28, 1 Semestre 1996. Pgs.154-177.

Casanova, Jacques. *The Memoirs of Jacques Casanova de Seingalt: Venetian Years.* transl. by Arthur Machen. New York: G. P. Putnam's Sons. 1902.

Davis, Robert C. *The War of the Fists: Pop Culture*

and Public Violence in Late Renaissance Venice. New York: Oxford University Press, 1994.

Donatelli, Carlo. *The Gondola: An Extraordinary Naval Architecture.* Venice: Arsenale Editrice, 1994.

Fraigneau, Andre. *The Venice I Love.* translated by Ruth Whipple Fermaud. New York: Tudor Publishing Company, 1959.

"The Gondola." pamphlet. Museo Storico Navale. Venezia: Italia. March 1997.

Honour, Hugh. *The Companion Guide to Venice.* New York: Harper and Row Publishers, 1996.

"In Gondola per Venezia." pamphlet. Venice: Instituzione per la Conservatione della Gondola e la Tutella del Gondoliere, May 1997.

James, Henry. *Italian Hours.* New York: The Ecco Press, 1987.

Lane, Frederic C. *Venice: A Maritime Republic.* Baltimore: The Johns Hopkins University Press, 1973.

Links, J.G. *Venice for Pleasure.* fifth revised edition. Wakefield: Moyer Bell, 1995.

Littlewood, Ian. *A Literary Companion to Venice.* New York: St. Martin's Griffin, 1991.

Mann, Thomas. *Death in Venice and Seven Other Stories.* translated by H.T. Lowe-Porter. New York: Vintage Books, 1930.

McCarthy, Mary. *Venice Observed.* San Diego: A Harvest Book, 1963.

Miller, John and Kirsten, ed. *Chronicles Abroad: Venice.* San Francisco: Chronicle Books, 1994.

Morris, Jan. *Venice.* 3rd revised edition. London: Faber and Faber, 1993.

Morris, Wright. *Love Affair-A Venetian Journal.* New York: Harper and Row, Publishers, 1972.

Penzo, Giberto, with the collaboration of Saverio Pastor. *Forcole, Remi e Voga alla Veneta.* Venice: Il Leggio Libreria Editrice, 1997.

Quennell, Peter. *Byron in Italy.* London: Collins Publishers, 1941.

Rowdon, Maurice. *The Silver Age of Venice.* New York: Praeger Publishing, 1970.

Theroux, Paul. *The Great Railway Bazaar.* Boston: Houghton Mifflin Company, 1975.

Twain, Mark. *The Innocents Abroad.* New York: Signet Classic, 1966.

Vidal, Gore. *Vidal in Venice.* New York: Summit Books, 1987.

Vittorio, Eugenio. *El Gondolero y su Gondola.* Venezia: Editorial Evi, 1979.

Voelkel, Dr. Theodore S. "Venice City Fact Sheet." ACIS pamphlet. Boston: 1994.

Kathleen Ann González started out as a teacher but was suprised to find that she was a writer and photographer as well. While she spends most of the year trying to infect teenagers with her great enthusiasm for literature, she still squeezes in time to write about her work, her students and her travels. She has published several essays and short stories over the years and has hopes for a future publication of her collection of poetry.